KARDASHIAN

Konfidential

EXCLUSIVE NEW PHOTOGRAPHY
FOR THIS BOOK BY
NICK SAGLIMBENI

KARDASHIAN
Konfidential

BY
KOURTNEY, KIM, AND KHLOÉ
KARDASHIAN

St. Martin's Press

NEW YORK

www.stmartins.com

INTERIOR EXECUTED BY DOWNTOWN BOOKWORKS INC.

Interior design by Georgia Rucker Design

ISBN 978-0-312-62807-9

First Edition: November 2010

10 9 8 7 6 5 4 3 2 1

DEDICATION

We want to dedicate our book to our father. Dad, without you, we know we would not be the women we are today. We know that every blessing in our lives is because you are our angel watching over us. This book is just a glimpse of what you have blessed us with. We know your spirit has guided us through every challenge, highlight, and memory we have had. We miss you more than we did yesterday and less than we will tomorrow. We are sisters because of you. We love you, Daddy.

CONTENTS

ACKNOWLEDGMENTS

Thanks to everyone who made this book possible:

Our "momager," the fabulous Kris Jenner, and the rest of our wonderful family: Rob Kardashian, Bruce Jenner, Kendall Jenner, Kylie Jenner, Scott Disick, Mason Disick, and Lamar Odom. We wouldn't be able to live without you guys. You are our heart and soul.

The incomparable Lisa DuFort, who keeps Kris's office running smoothly. Our book agent, the amazing Michael Broussard, and his colleagues at ISB New Media, Greg Ray and Michelle Lemmons. Our superstar publicists, Jill Fritzo and Noelle Keshishian. Photographer Nick Saglimbeni and everyone at SlickForce Studios for gorgeous pictures, including this book's cover! Writer, Robin Micheli. Ted Harbert, Lisa Berger, Damla Dogan, Jason Sarlanis, and John Rizzotti at E!. Ryan Seacrest; John Murray, Melissa Bidwell, Farnaz Farjam, and Jeff Jenkins, and the entire staff at Bunim/Murray Productions; and Jennifer Haughton and Janie Marcus at Buzz Media, for helping us with our websites. Monica Rose, our phenomenal stylist. Our amazing Glam Squad who keeps us looking fab: Joyce Bonelli, Mario Dedivanovic, Frank Galasso, Clyde Haygood, Maiesha Oliver, Frankie Payne, Mary Phillips, Rob Scheppy, Rob Talty, and Phillip Wolff. We are also grateful to our DASH dolls, who help us run our clothing business: Roya Bahrami, Brittaney Minton, Josefina Wytrykusz; and our cousin CiCi Bussey. And all the girls who make our lives livable: Sheiva Ghasemzade, Malika Haqq, and Sydney Hitchcock.

Thank you also to Julie Merberg, LeeAnn Pemberton, Patty Brown, Sarah Parvis, and Pam Abrams at Downtown Bookworks; and Georgia Rucker at Georgia Rucker Design for the design of the book's interior. And last but not at all least, thanks to everyone at St. Martin's Press: our brilliant editor, Elizabeth Beier; her blazingly efficient assistant, Michelle Richter; COO Steve Cohen; publishers Sally Richardson and Matthew Shear; the hardworking production team Karen Gillis, Eric Gladstone, Amelie Littell, Eric Meyer, and James Sinclair—this wouldn't be an actual book without you!; Michael Storrings, Ervin Serrano, and Lisa Pompilio for the gorgeous cover design; John Murphy, Ann Day, and Loren Jaggers in Publicity; and Matt Baldacci and Nancy Trypuc in Marketing.

Kardashian
Konfidential

INTRODUCTION

Once upon a time there were three sisters...

The oldest sister, Kourtney Mary, was born April 18, 1979. The middle sister, Kimberly Noel, was born the very next year, on October 21, 1980. And on June 27, 1984, their baby sister Khloé Alexandra was born.

When the sisters were little, they played together and had fun and loved each other very much. Their life was like a fairy tale!

Then the sisters grew up, but they still played together and had fun and loved each other very much.

My mom ALWAYS (and I do mean always) dressed us alike at the holidays. I might have been three here. I was always a tall person so you can't go by the way I look! — *Khloé*

This was at the London Hotel meeting with all of the International E! team. We all randomly wore glitzy sparkly dresses and looked like a music group! — *Kim*

Of course, as in all good fairy tales, they encountered some troubles along the way. But they stayed positive and relied on each other and their family. And they always worked hard to make their dreams come true.

Then one day, the sisters woke up to find that they were not only rich and beautiful and blessed with a loving family, but famous—or

That's our storybook tale, which is actually the real-life story of us, the Kardashian sisters. Bible!* Our life really was like a fairy tale when we were kids growing up. We had the most spectacular birthday parties ever. We were very fortunate to have parents who believed in a strong family bond. They provided us with a lot of material things but they also taught us to appreciate what we had and be responsible and work hard.

Of course, not everything was perfect. (Our story definitely has a few sad parts!) But in rough times, we always rely on each other, and our family, to pull through.

And then, when we grew up . . . well, you kind of know what happened then. Some people say it all started with Kim's bootylicious butt. Whatever. One thing led to another and suddenly we were starring in *Keeping Up with the Kardashians*. And then *Kourtney and Khloé Take Miami*. And the shows led to other great opportunities, and now we've been on magazine covers and talk shows and have our own clothing and jewelry and skin care lines. Sometimes it seems like we're everywhere at once!

On TV, we've let you and millions of other people be right there with us while we've experienced some very private moments. Getting married. Giving birth. Dealing with men. Crying on camera. Fighting with our mom—and each other. Confronting a crisis or two or three.

You may think you know everything about us by now.

Trust us, dolls, you don't!

There's a lot more to the Kardashian sisters than what's been caught on tape. Way more. And because we absolutely love and cherish you all—our incredible fans—we've decided to share everything with you.

First of all—hello!—we were the Kardashian sisters all those years before you began *Keeping Up* with us. All sorts of things happened when we were kids and teenagers that made us who we are. We're gonna give you the whole scoop about growing up and everything that went on in

*KARDASHIONARY DEFINITION

BIBLE **A promise word we say a lot.**

DERIVATION: Our dad wouldn't let us swear when we were growing up. So instead of saying "swear to God" we'd say "Bible." A boyfriend of Kim's came up with it. We had other promise words with our friends, too. Like Kim had a friend in art class and instead of saying "swear to God!" or "Bible!" they'd say, "Art!"

our family. We want you to know about our amazing dad, Robert Kardashian, who we love and miss so much. And about how Bruce Jenner, our mom's second husband, became such an important part of our family. (One of us—we won't mention any names, at least for now—really gave him a hard time at first!!) We're also going to tell you all about the rest of our ginormous clan. And what it's really like to be a celebrity.

We'll fill you in on all of it, good and bad. Because honestly, it's not all glam and glitz. It *is* a lot of fun, but it's a lot of long hours, too, and sometimes we get exhausted. Like when we film for eighteen hours straight and then go make an appearance somewhere and finally go to bed at 2:30 in the morning and have to get up four hours later for hair and makeup and start all over again! We've learned how to deal with the challenges, though, and we're not complaining. The perks we enjoy are fab, and we're really grateful for them. So we'll take you along for an inside peek at some of our more exciting adventures in the limelight.

Plus we want to give you an idea of all the stuff that goes on when the cameras aren't rolling, when we're just being sisters, or

We used to have to get all dolled up and take black-and-white photos for our Christmas cards each year. I think I was about ten years old here. *Love* that we have these! — *Kourtney*

hanging with our friends. You know, private time. Sometimes it's actually more interesting than what turns up on the show.

We'll even let you in on some secrets that we've picked up along the way. Tips about makeup and clothes and how to look your best, of course, but not just that. We've learned a lot living our crazy lives. Maybe what we've discovered can help you in your own crazy lives.

Yes, we've been pampered. We've led a charmed life. Sometimes we still really feel like we're living a fairy tale!

But fairy tales only go so far. We believe in creating our own good fortune. Our parents drilled it into us from the time we were little girls that we were ultimately responsible for ourselves. They made it clear that if we wanted to lead enchanted lives, it would be

up to us to make it all happen. We might have complained about it when we were younger but now we're so glad they raised us that way. We work hard for what we have, and we believe in girl power.

This was around Thanksgiving at our school in Beverly Hills when Kourtney was about six and I was five. I used to follow her and copy everything she did! — *Kim*

That's right, girl power. You don't have to be born into a fairy tale. Sure, it helps to have certain advantages. But in the end, you're pretty much just like us—you have to find out what works for you, and make the most of it. You have to be disciplined and organized and fierce. With confidence and commitment, you can make your own dreams come true.

So, dolls, to sum it up: We're going to share it all with you. The glamour, the grind, the thrills, the spills, the inside story of all things Kardashian. Right now, in these pages. In our own words.

Bible!

Love,
Kourtney, Kim, Khloé

Kourtney

Astrology Sign: ARIES

Arians tend to be courageous, confident, domineering, and sometimes selfish. They are competitive and stay focused on their best interests. Ideally suited to be an entrepreneur. "In other words, bossy—I'm definitely that. Though I only insist on something if I really care; otherwise, I'm happy to go along."

Known for her . . .

. . . unpredictable relationship with the father of her child, and for giving birth by pulling her own baby out into the world.

Believes she's . . .

. . . the most confident of the sisters.

Her sisters say she's . . .

. . . laid-back, calm, collected, rational, unemotional, the strongest of the three.

Thinks you've never lived until . . .

. . . you have a baby in your life! "For me, the experience has changed my heart and soul, adding such a different level of love and happiness and making me live in a whole new way."

Wants you to know . . .

. . . she realizes that relationship drama makes good TV. "I'm not stupid. It's not interesting for us to be sitting there getting along."

Never leaves home without . . .

. . . her BlackBerry, her wallet, and "a little bit of fashion!"

Is often heard saying . . .

. . . "I feel like." Or "Mmm, yeah, yeah . . ."

Is the one most likely to . . .

. . . walk away from it all someday and never look back; become a fashion mogul.

Kim

Astrology Sign: LIBRA

Librans seek balance, and are usually tactful and romantic, crave attention from partners, and can be self-indulgent. They are excellent organizers and planners and make good diplomats. "I don't like confrontations, and I'm very big on planning. And of course I'm in love with being in love!"

Known for her . . .

. . . bounteous booty, tendency to cry, role as the family princess.

Believes she's . . .

. . . the most considerate of the sisters.

Her sisters say she's . . .

. . . sweet, shy, hard-working, dramatic, the most emotional of the three.

Thinks you've never lived until . . .

. . . you've loved with all your heart and soul!

Wants you to know . . .

. . . she loves to flirt but is only interested in long-term relationships.

Never leaves home without . . .

. . . her BlackBerry, her Amex black card, big sunglasses, and always some type of candy.

Is often heard saying . . .

. . . "Oh my God! That is so amazing!" Or "Do you like this? It's so me!"

Is the one most likely to . . .

. . . fall in love dozens of times, work every single day of her life, go the extra mile to please her fans.

Khloé

Astrology Sign: CANCER

Cancers are nurturing, unpredictable, and fragile—beneath a tough exterior—though sometimes temperamental. Skilled at judging a person's true intentions, they can excel in a wide range of occupations. "I have a hard shell on the outside, but inside I'm soft as pie."

Known for her . . .

. . . wicked wit, colorful language, and whirlwind romance.

Believes she's . . .

. . . the most street-smart of the sisters.

Her sisters say she's . . .

. . . tough on the outside but sensitive inside, generous, affectionate, the most fun of the three.

Thinks you've never lived until . . .

. . . you've truly experienced love.

Wants you to know . . .

. . . "I'm an old soul. I really like old movies and other things that were way before my time."

Never leaves home without . . .

. . . her wedding ring, her BlackBerry, her credit card, face powder. "I'm an Armenian and I get oily!"

Is often heard saying . . .

. . . "It's to die!" Or "Amen!"

Is the one most likely to . . .

. . . surprise you, become a talk show host, make you really regret it if you hurt Kourtney or Kim.

THE WAY WE TALK:
A GLOSSARY TO K-SPEAK

We don't have a secret language or anything. But we do have a few expressions that we use a lot, so this will help you understand us!

AMAZE: Amazing.

AMEN: Thank you! or That's the truth.

BIBLE!: "I swear! Swear to God!"

BIBLE?: "Really? *Do* you swear to God?"

DOLL: An endearing word for our friends.

DOUCHELORD: Any guy that is not worthy or mean to the sistahs.

KHLO-MONEY: A nickname for Khloé.

MOMAGER: Someone who's your mom *and* your manager.

THE PEAK AND THE PIT: A discussion-starter in which everyone takes turns talking about the best and worst of their day.

PREACH: "For sure! Amen!"

RIDIC: Ridiculous

SHADY: Suspicious, not quite right, like something's up.

SISTAHS: Sisters, of course.

SICK: Fantastic, that is when it doesn't just mean sick, as in ill.

SLORE: A slut and a whore.

TO DIE: Short for "to die for."

TOTES, OR TOTES MAGOTES: "Totally!"

This is me at four, Kourtney, and NaNa (my dad's mom) in the driveway of the house we grew up in. Our fish had died and we buried him that day, right behind us in the dirt. — *Kim*

1

TOWER LANE

The three of us grew up in a big house in Beverly Hills. We always called the house "Tower Lane" because that's the street it was on. It even sounds like it belongs in a fairy tale, doesn't it?

The house was at the end of a private road on a cul de sac, with a really long driveway. We had a pool that was shaped like a duck, and the jacuzzi was shaped like an egg—at least that's the way it looked from the upstairs windows of the house. We had a tennis court and a pool house with a bar that we called the tennis house, because it had all these racquets in there.

We used to take tennis lessons, but the best time we had on the court was running around playing and spraying each other with the water hose. Our friends used to come over for tennis lessons and swimming lessons, and our mom would bring out iced tea and Girl Scout cookies. Our house was definitely the place to be. Those times will be embedded in our minds forever; they made us feel so happy and grand!

In the back of our house we had a forest—well, it seemed like a forest back then—and we used to build our forts out there. We had a swing set with a really long swing. A spooky guy who looked like "Daddy" Warbucks lived next door. He had llamas and peacocks that would just run around all over his yard. Kourtney used to shoot slingshots through his fence but swears she didn't hit any of his animals. There were only three houses on our cul de sac and Bruce Springsteen lived on one side of us. Then later he bought the spooky guy's house, too, so we were surrounded on all sides by Bruce Springsteen. And Jay Leno lived down the street. We always saw him with his vintage cars when we walked our dogs.

We had lots of animals: cats named Coco and Chanel, hamsters, huge turtles who always got lost on the property. There was a woodpecker that always knocked on the window of Dad's office. Kourtney even kept four white mice called Eenie, Meanie, Miney, and Moe! It was horrible when Valentina, our little bichon frise, ate snail poison at a neighbor's house and died. Kim and Kourtney shared a room then and could hear each other sniffling and crying over it at night. We also had two big Dobermans with Armenian names, Sarkus and Anush. Whenever we wanted our friends to leave, we'd let out the Dobermans. Everyone would get so scared they'd run out and call their parents to pick them up!

This is my mom and dad's first trip together to Hawaii. They look so young and happy! — Kim

Our mom and dad first met in San Diego. She was seventeen and working as a flight attendant. He was eleven years older and studying law at the University of California at San Diego. They both happened to go to the Del Mar Racetrack one day. Our dad got one of his female friends to introduce herself to Mom. Then the plan was for the friend to introduce Mom to Dad—and it worked. They actually didn't start dating until about a year later. Our dad definitely pursued our mom, not the other way around. But they were both really fun people, so they were drawn to each other, and four years after they began dating, they got married.

Then the following year, when Mom was twenty-three, she had Kourtney. Apparently the woman was born to breed, because at twenty-four she had Kim, and Khloé came along three years later and Rob the year after that. Then she started up all over again and had Kendall when she was forty and Kylie at forty-two.

Our parents just loved to entertain and have people over—and people just loved coming over to be entertained! Tower Lane was truly party central. On weekends we'd have huge barbecues with our friends and our grandparents and aunts and uncles and cousins. The grownups would play tennis and we'd lay out in the sun. Eighties music like Michael Jackson and Luther Vandross would be blasting everywhere.

I love this. It was in Hawaii and my mom was nineteen. She is really beautiful. — *Kim*

This is one of my favorite pictures! I was eight so Kourtney was nine, and Khloé was five. — *Kim*

The parties we had at our house were totally amazing. Seriously, our parents were known for throwing the coolest parties ever. Everything was an event for them. Mom is such a social butterfly, she knows how to throw a party in like two seconds and it'll be the best one you've ever been to. When we were little, our parents always had a scavenger hunt on New Year's Eve. Their friends would meet at our house and then they'd have to go out and find little objects and things, such as a matchbook from the Beverly Hills Hotel, and then race back to our house before midnight.

One year for the New Year's Eve party we had cancan dancers, so the invitations Mom sent out were actual life-size chocolate legs!

Mom also liked to throw surprise birthday parties. She would go *so* over the top. It was great. We'd have pony rides and petting zoos at our house, or clowns, or all these people dressed up as cartoon characters. One time, at Kim's thirteenth birthday party, the dog ate the cake. The next year Kim got to have her party at Neverland, because she dated Michael Jackson's nephew, so twenty of us rode up to Santa Barbara in a big van. There were amusement park rides and movies and a zoo with baby elephants, definitely her most memorable party ever.

We had awesome birthday parties from the get-go. Big Bird came to our house for Kourtney's first birthday party. Not that Kourtney technically remembers, of course, but she's seen it on video.

We have practically our entire childhoods on video. Hey, maybe that's why it's so natural for us to live so much of our lives on camera with our TV show! Dad was absolutely glued to his video camera when we were kids. Everything we did, he documented it. It's very cool. We each have tapes and we watch them a lot, especially now that our dad is gone. It's fun, but it's kinda sad that we never get to see him. He was always holding the camera, filming. But at least we do get to hear him talking.

From the beginning, our parents taught us the huge importance of family. We always had dinner together. And we were never allowed to talk on the phone during dinner. Every night we did this thing called The Peak and the Pit. Our dad always started. You'd go around the table and

> I love to entertain and one day I was rushing around so my mom was a sweetheart and to help me out, she made her amazing guacamole that she's famous for. She's incredibly thoughtful and always thinks five steps ahead, and she just wanted to make sure I had enough chips. :) — *Khloé*

Bunny !
You need
more chips!!!
don't forget
guacamole !
i love you
mommy xoxo

10-23-97
Khloé
I love you
more than
you will ever
know. You are
my sunshine.
mommy xoxo
♡

> I love the way my mom and dad would always write these really sweet notes of love to us. — *Khloé*

everybody had to say what the peak and the pit of their day was—you know, the best and the worst.

One time, later on after we moved out of Tower Lane, we were having dinner with these really good friends of our parents and we did The Peak and the Pit. When it was Kim's turn she said, "Well, the pit of my day was getting two traffic tickets because I went through two stop signs—but the peak of my day is being here with all of you because now my dad won't yell at me!" We don't do The Peak and the Pit as often anymore, but we do it for special occasions like Khloés wedding.

Dad always got really involved in our lives, much more than a lot of our friends' dads. He always wanted to do stuff with us and was interested in our friends. He'd ask us, "What homework do you have?" and then tell us when it was time to go do it. He knew what was going on at school, and he'd follow up with us, remembering to ask things like, "How did you do on your spelling test?" And he came to all our soccer games. He even coached us for a while. Our mom was really involved, too. She used to take us everywhere with her and she was even the leader of Kourtney's Brownie troops. That's why we like the movie *Troop Beverly Hills* so much, because we swear, that was just like our mom!

There was always music in the house, which was completely wired with a stereo system. Our dad liked to listen to music everywhere, even in the bathroom. He was completely into doo-wop. We'd always listen to this fifties tape with songs like "Soldier Boy," "Lollipop," and "Who Put the Bomp?"

We took fun vacations. For spring break we usually went to Mexico, and

That's my grandmother MJ and Kris with all of us in 1985. Each of our faces says so much about our personalities. — *Kourtney*

every Easter we went to Palm Springs. Sometimes we'd go to Hawaii. We always ate Thanksgiving dinner in a restaurant, because for as far back as we can remember we always went skiing in Vail every Thanksgiving with our family and some friends. We used to rent a house with an indoor swimming pool. The adults had a hot tub and at night they played a game from a book of questions, which was all about sex. They thought we were in bed, but really we were hiding out eavesdropping!

One thing we really appreciated as kids was the way our parents always valued our opinions. Our dad would want to hear what you had to say, and he'd truly take it into consideration. It made you feel like a person, and a respected part of the family. That probably has a lot to do with why we're so free to express our opinions with one another today. Even when we're screaming them!

Sometimes we kids would fight with one another, of course. But if we ever said things like "I hate you!" our mom would always call us on it: "No, you cannot ever say that to your sister! She's your sister and you have to love her. She's part of your family and the most important thing in the world is your family!"

People have mentioned to us they notice we say "I love you" all the time to each other. It's true. Even Rob does, which is nice because sometimes guys think they're too cool for that. We all think it's normal and natural and we've always said it.

But probably we exchange I love yous more since our dad died. He used to say it all the time to us. He'd never get off the phone without an "I love you" and we all still do that with each other.

We think it's a good idea to say "I love you" as often as possible. You never know what could happen. If you love someone, make sure they know you do!

FASHION FAUX PAS
◄◄ KIM ►►

Sometimes Kourtney liked to embarrass me when we were little. One time we were looking at a magazine and she said, "Kim, do you know all these models' names?" I didn't, of course. So she pointed to ads for different jeans and said, "This model is named Jordache. This one's named Calvin." Like that. Then her friends came over and she asked me to recite the names of the models and I go, "Jordache, Calvin . . . " She said, "Isn't Kim so dumb?" They all laughed and I started to cry.

BEDTIME STORIES

Kourtney: Our dad read to us a lot when we were little kids. My mom saved all those books, and now we're going to pass them on to Mason—at least until he has brothers or sisters or cousins to share them with!

Curious George: *Our dad really loved that one.*

Thingumajig Book of Do's and Don'ts: *This was a book on manners.*

Mother Goose: *Of course!*

Dr. Seuss: *Especially* Oh, the Places You'll Go!

Goodnight Moon: *It's so adorable!*

CRUISIN'

Khloé: Dad had a Mercedes convertible two-seater and he used to drive me and Rob around with the top down. There was just a little strip between the two seats and you weren't supposed to sit there, but Dad let us. If he saw a cop, he'd shout, "Duck!" And then even when there wasn't a cop, he'd shout, "Duck!" because he was so silly. He liked to have fun. I remember he'd be playing his fifties music in his Mercedes and he'd quiz me, "What's this song called, Khloé?" We don't really like that fifties stuff all the time but we do listen to it when we want to get in the spirit of our dad. And I picked up his musical taste in old-school R&B, like Aretha Franklin and Donny Hathaway and Anita Baker.

KIMMY AND KOURTNEY AND LITTLE BABY KHLOÉ

KOURTNEY: When Khloé was born, we were so excited, and we would always hold her. We were dying to see what she would look like when she got older. It was like, "Khloé, please, please, just grow up so we can find out!" Because she looked so different from the rest of us.

KIM: She had blond, curly hair and green eyes. The rest of us are all dark, and we're hairy, like most Armenians. We could just hardly wait to see!

KHLOÉ: And I never even thought they cared.

KIM: I really loved to torture her. I'd dress her up and insist on picking her up against her will. I would just drag her around like a doll while she screamed and cried. It was partly because I always wanted to be the center of attention. I was always like, "Take a picture of me!"

KOURTNEY: And remember, Khloé, I apologized to you for this when you were about sixteen, because I felt so bad about it for so many years. I used to go into your nursery and I guess I was jealous that you were getting all this attention and I would say all these mean horrible things to you. You were just a tiny newborn, and everyone could hear me on the baby monitor, too!

This was my father's favorite photo of me. He had it in his office right by his computer in the same frame ever since it was taken when I was five. I don't remember why I was so upset at the time, but as you can see I've always had an expressive face! — *Khloé*

KHLOÉ: It's so weird you felt guilty for so long and I don't even remember it. I do remember one time I went to wake up Kim to show her what I got from the tooth fairy, and she said, "You're so stupid, don't you know that Mom's the tooth fairy?" Sometimes the two of you would just crush my dreams like that.

KOURTNEY: You had this crazy energy, Khloé, and you were always laughing and running around. I remember for a while you thought you were a dog. You'd crawl around and bark at people and even lick people's legs.

KHLOÉ: Yes, I've always been a bitch!

KIM: You and Rob used to play together when you were little.

KHLOÉ: Yes, but we fought like cats and dogs, so to speak.

KOURTNEY: Back then you were attached to Mom at the hip.

KHLOÉ: I know, I was completely obsessed with Mom at one point. That's when you two were really close.

KOURTNEY: Yeah, Khloé, you were always off with Mom while Kim and I were doing things.

KHLOÉ: You two were like twins!

KIM: I do feel like Kourtney and I really grew up together. I followed Kourtney everywhere.

KOURTNEY: Kim was my little sidekick. We did everything together. I called her Kimbo sometimes. Wherever I went, she'd come along and whatever I was doing, she'd do it, too. One time I remember I made you help me rearrange a shelf of books from tallest to smallest.

KIM: I would just copy you. And you would torture me and boss me around. You'd say, "Kim, you have to say you want this for dinner because this is what I want." And I'd say, "Okay!" I was your little puppet. Remember when we'd play and you'd pretend to be Donna Karan?

KOURTNEY: And you had to be my assistant, and I'd order you around.

KIM: You'd say, "Do this and this and that!" And finally I would start whining, "Kourtney, I don't want to play anymore!"

KOURTNEY: But I'd tell you, "That's what an assistant does! You have to do this! Get to work!"

KHLOÉ: You used to be evil, Kourtney!

SO ARMENIAN

If you've watched our show you probably know that we're Armenian. I guess we talk about it a lot. That's probably because being Armenian was a really big thing to our dad. His heritage was so important to him and he wanted us to know where we came from. A lot of people think our mom might be Armenian, because she's dark. She's actually of Scottish and Dutch descent. But she was always a good sport and went along with the Armenian thing in our family.

Here are Kourt and me right after Easter services. She was 3 and I was only 1 1/2. We're with our grandparents on our dad's side. — *Kim*

Our dad didn't speak a lot of Armenian but he went to an Armenian school when he was a kid and always told us Armenian stories. We love that we're Armenian. When Mason was born, Kim immediately said, "Oh, he looks so Armenian!" After Kourtney had Mason, she took him to visit our grandfather, our dad's dad, in an Armenian nursing home. She found him chatting with all the nurses in Armenian. We didn't know until then that he could speak the language so fluently. Our dad made it a point to give money to that nursing home; there's a plaque on the wall there with his name on it.

When we were kids, our dad sometimes used to add "Jon" to our names, because in Armenian, "Jon" means "dear." So it was KourtneyJon, KimJon, KhloéJon. And he was always going to Armenian people if he needed something done. Like if the car had to be repaired, he'd go to an Armenian mechanic. He was very respected in the Armenian community in L.A.

When we were kids our grandparents lived in Century City. Our NaNa had our entire family (her three children and all of her grandchildren) over to their Century City condo all the time for *bishi*. *Bishi* is an Armenian breakfast that only NaNa could make. You have to make the dough the night before so it can rise. Early the next morning, you roll the dough into flat pieces and fry it. Kourtney is the only one in the family who can make it now. On special occasions she makes the dough and Khloé does the frying.

Every year, either on Dad's birthday or on the anniversary of the day he passed, we go to his favorite Armenian restaurant, called the Carousel. We've never been to Armenia, but someday we'd like to go. When we started our jewelry line, we wanted it to honor our Armenian heritage somehow, so we used Armenian symbols in the designs. It's very cool. We learned a lot about our culture doing it and now other people can learn about our culture, too.

FROM NANA'S RECIPE BOX

We were going to give you NaNa's recipe for *bishi* but our mom wouldn't let us. She says it's a secret family recipe. But we can give you a recipe NaNa wrote out by hand for these Armenian cookies that are to die!

This should make about 3 dozen —

Simit Cookies

5½ cups of flour
3 tsp. baking powder
3/4 cup of sugar
(mix together)
well

add 2 beaten eggs to above

melt together (beaten)
1 cup milk
½ pound (not salted)
oleo (Fleischmans)
½ c. mezzon oil
over

when heated + melted add to above and blend well

after all is blended (well) like dough for bread or cookies.

Roll out like long hot dog. Make into (inches) "8"

Brush with egg (beaten) sprinkle with sesame seed
10 minutes bake til brown —
375° til brown —
I usualy cook one sheet bottom rack — then put bottom on top rack — for 10 minutes til brown —

24

WHEN
I GROW UP...

My mom always dressed Kim and me alike. This is from Christmas when I was 3 and Kim was only 1 1/2. — *Kourtney*

Kourtney: Even when I was little I loved clothes and shopping, and I wanted to be a fashion designer. One year when I got older my parents gave me a sewing machine and in high school I would buy patterns and fabrics. One year when my mom was getting ready for her famous Christmas Eve party that night, I saw a Jill Stuart dress in a magazine that I was dying over. It was a little lavender mini-dress, all ruffly, and it was really for spring, but I just had to have it. So I went to the fabric store and came home and made it and wore it to the party that night.

Kim: I always wanted to be a reality TV star. When *The Real World* first came out on MTV I told my friend Allison, "When we get old enough let's make an audition tape!" She said she didn't want to be on *Real World* but instead she would be my manager. And it's so funny because now she's one of the biggest managers in the music business. And it turned out that the company that produces both of our shows for E! is the one that created and still produces *The Real World*!

Khloé: When I was young I fantasized about being a Victoria's Secret model. Because back in those days they were the only models who were allowed to have boobs and a butt. Everyone else was skinny skinny.

2

FAMILY FEUDS AND OTHER STICKY STUFF

*E*verything seemed pretty perfect in our lives until our parents got a divorce. It was sad for Kim but it didn't really faze Khloé, who was only five and didn't really understand what was going on. (Rob had absolutely no idea because he was just two!) It was the hardest on Kourtney, who was the oldest. Especially when Mom remarried so soon after.

Kimberly
I took your barbie P.J. and I want to wear them on friday call me at mommy's if yes or no.

Our dad remained a major part of our lives. We would go back and forth from our mom's to our dad's. Usually we'd be ten days at our mom's and then go spend five days at our dad's. They both made a big effort to make sure we were always their first priority. Neither one of them tried to win us over from the other one; they presented a united front and supported each other as parents. It took a while, and some work, but they did a good job at becoming good friends, better friends even than some married couples.

Family values were always so important in our home. In a weird way, the divorce actually strengthened them for us. It brought a new dimension to our family values and made us aware of them at a young age. To see how mature our parents were set a good example, and then when our mom and dad and even Bruce got along so well, it showed us even more ways of loving one another as family. Our dad always said, "Everything happens for a reason." Even when he was dying, he said, "That's why Bruce is here now, to take care of you after I'm gone."

Bruce came into our lives right after our parents separated. Mom met him on a blind date, they instantly fell in love, and they got married just five months later. We were so excited that he had four kids the same ages as us. We thought, "How cool, we have this huge family," though Kourtney didn't adjust very well to Bruce, at first.

A few years or so after the divorce our family went through an experience that altered our lives forever. It was after Dad sold the house on Tower Lane and moved to Encino, in the Valley, to the northwest over the hill from Beverly Hills. It was around the time Kourtney was starting high school and began living there most of the time.

You know the football player O.J. Simpson? If you don't, it's because his gridiron glory days were before our time, in the 1970s, but he was one of the best running backs in the NFL. And he was charming and good-looking, and after football he did some commercials and movies. If you haven't seen him in *Airplane*, you're really missing something!

OUR DAD ALWAYS SAID, "EVERYTHING HAPPENS FOR A REASON." EVEN WHEN HE *WAS* DYING, HE SAID, "THAT'S WHY BRUCE IS HERE NOW, TO TAKE CARE OF YOU AFTER I'M GONE."

28

O.J. was our dad's best friend in college, and we were all close to his family. We called him Uncle O.J. One of our mom's best friends was his wife, Nicole, and we grew up with their kids. We would even spend spring breaks together.

Then Nicole was killed, and O.J. was accused of her murder. One of our dad's best traits was fierce loyalty. So he renewed his attorney's license—he used to be a lawyer before he became a businessman—and helped defend O.J. All through that time, O.J. stayed at our dad's house, in the room that was Khloé's bedroom. There was a famous car chase where O.J. was speeding down the freeway for hours in a white Bronco with the police pursuing him; the whole country stopped what it was doing to watch. That car chase started at our dad's house, and our dad was on national TV reading the note that O.J. had left behind. It was so surreal!

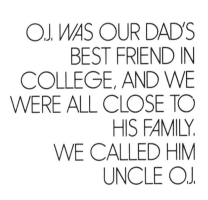

O.J. WAS OUR DAD'S BEST FRIEND IN COLLEGE, AND WE WERE ALL CLOSE TO HIS FAMILY. WE CALLED HIM UNCLE O.J.

People felt very strongly about the O.J. case. We were still pretty young then—Khloé was nine or ten at the time—and for us it was difficult because it was the first time our family had ever been divided. In a way, it was worse than the divorce.

Our mom was 100 percent convinced that O.J. had killed Nicole, and of course, my dad was on O.J.'s side. It's not like they made us take sides, but whenever we were at my mom's house, you just knew that if you talked about what Dad thought, Mom would get really mad. And you didn't really want to talk about what Mom thought at Dad's house, either. We kind of believed O.J. at the time but it was just us taking our dad's side more than anything. Mom had already gotten married and our dad was by himself. We felt bad for him and we were supporting him. It was extremely stressful.

And it was scary sometimes, too, even dangerous. People camped outside the house, not just media but people who were only there because they were angry. A lot of them got nasty, and our dad said the phone was tapped. We got bomb threats, and one former policeman told Dad he was going to hurt us kids, so Dad always told us to be very aware of who was around us or who might be following us. One time we were kicked out of a restaurant because they didn't want our dad there. Some of our friends' parents stopped letting them come over to our house.

There was a guy one time on the street, who just started cussing out

Dad, swearing and calling him terrible names. Dad got so mad, he said, "How dare you say those things to me when I'm with my daughters!?" And he started chasing the guy. One time, though, someone keyed the word *guilty* on Dad's black Tahoe, and Khloé cried and cried. We're pretty sure our dad never let on to us everything that was happening. He always protected us.

Usually we could go over to Dad's house whenever we wanted, but Mom didn't want us staying there a lot then, even with Kourtney living there. Dad used to come over to Mom's house lots of times to eat with all of us, including Bruce. Bruce and Dad would even play golf together! But not during the O.J. trial.

After the murder, we used to go see O.J. and Nicole's kids Sydney and Justin in Orange County, where they lived with Nicole's family, the Browns. Our mom is still close to the Browns and we stay in touch with the kids, but we haven't seen them much since they moved to Florida with their dad. When people ask us our opinions of the trial or the outcome, we don't answer. We choose to leave that in the past and not revisit the emotions from a painful period in our lives. It was a really hard time for our family and definitely was part of what shaped our characters.

DAD USED TO COME OVER TO MOM'S HOUSE LOTS OF TIMES TO EAT WITH ALL OF US, INCLUDING BRUCE. BRUCE AND DAD WOULD EVEN PLAY GOLF TOGETHER!

i just KNEW

Kim: I had a weird feeling my parents were going to get divorced. My dad called a family meeting and I thought something must be going on because he had only ever called a family meeting once before. The divorce was hardest on Dad, because my mom was the one who initiated it. She was young and confused. We all felt really bad for him. And I felt bad for Kourtney because I saw her having such a hard time. She was just miserable, especially when my mom remarried.

Maybe I didn't feel as bothered by the divorce because I was focusing my anxiety on what was happening to my body. Right around the time of my parents splitting up, I was starting to develop physically, and I was upset by it, because it seemed so early to me. I always had a big butt—but so did Kourtney, just not as big as mine. But that's not what bothered me. It was my boobs. They were definitely bigger than Kourtney's, and I was mortified that they were growing so much. I got a lot of attention from the older boys in school, which made me feel uncomfortable. When

Doesn't my dad look just like Rob in this picture? I was eight or nine then. That's our Aunt Barbara on the right. — *Kim*

I got a training bra in the fourth grade, one boy came by and snapped the back of my bra. It was so embarrassing, I hated it. I remember sitting in the bathtub during that time and crying, putting hot washcloths over my breasts to try to shrink them. I literally prayed to God, "Please don't let them grow any bigger!" My mom used to say, "Just wait. Someday you'll be happy with your curves." And she was right. Now I embrace my curves.

I'm sure other girls go through the same thing, being ashamed of their bodies, and I wish I could make them understand that they shouldn't be!

THE CLANS come out

Kourtney: My parents never fought until they were getting a divorce. I never heard them argue when we were growing up, not even one time. Once, they called us into a family meeting to tell us that our family friends were getting a divorce. And we were like, "A divorce? That's crazy!" We just didn't understand it.

My parents' divorce was hardest on me because I was oldest and understood the most. Divorce can be so traumatizing for kids, even though in some cases it's probably for the best. You just want your parents to be together forever and you don't want anything to change.

I sided with my dad and I acted out with my mom a lot. We got into screaming, hair-pulling fights. She would grab my arm, and then I would dig my nails into her hand to get it off. I feel like every time I was at my mom's we would just argue.

Once I decided to run away. But I only ran down the street to my friend's house, literally about half a block. Then I called my dad and said, "I need to get out of here!" Meaning Mom's house. He lived fifteen or twenty minutes away. So he picked me up, but then he took me back to my mom's! He said, "You need to stay here, and you can't be disrespectful to your mom. You have to go apologize to her!" And I thought, oh, so you're not on my side anymore!

I was the only one who didn't like Bruce at first. Just because of my dad, you know? I felt like I was betraying him if I was nice to Bruce. We used to have fights all the time. I was so stubborn—but Bruce was kind of stubborn, too, and we would get into these wars over any little thing. If he said something like, "You can't do this," I'd say, "You're not my dad!"

I remember he used to pick me up from summer school on his Harley and we'd ride down Sunset Boulevard and I used to be embarrassed for some reason. Of course now it seems cool. I finally just got to know him as a person instead of judging him like I always had, but it took me a long time, at least two years or more. It's too bad, because he has always been such a good stepdad to take us all in and he truly loves us. He would do anything for us. If I called him right now and said, "Bruce, come hang my drapes," he'd be right over! I mean, he's literally the nicest guy. We've been really lucky.

And now we have our youngest sisters, Kendall and Kylie, in our lives. So I think some things are just meant to happen.

PUMPED UP

Khloé: My very first memory of Bruce is at the house on Tower Lane when I was about five or six. My mom was still living there when she was separated. Bruce came over and he was wearing these Reebok Pump shoes. My dad wore sneakers and all that but I'd never seen shoes like Bruce's and I was fascinated by them. I just remember sitting on his feet and pumping his shoes full of air, and there was a release button so you could then let out all the air. I thought, this guy is so cool!

When we moved to Malibu awhile after Mom and Bruce got married, I became obsessed with bringing home animals I found on the street. I wanted to be a vet when I grew up and have an RV so I could pick up animals every day; I would even bring home a goat if I found one. I didn't though; it was mostly dogs and cats, and I would show up literally every week with at least one. None of them

I loved Bruce right from the start. I'm wearing pump Reebok's sneakers in this photo; I was six. I thought it was so cool that Bruce was sponsored by the company and he would get them for us. — *Khloé*

33

ever went to the pound, because my mom would always find good homes for them. But they didn't stay with us. Mom doesn't really care for dogs, or animals in general. She's just like Kim with animals: They're cute from a distance, but let's move on.

I was never a rodent person, but I did have some unusual pets—one time I brought home some chickens, which really annoyed Mom. Finally Mom got so frustrated with those chickens that I came home one day with a friend of mine and went to my room, and it was filled with chickens and chicken poop. Mom said, "Fine, you want chickens, they can live in your room!"

OLYMPIAN, HANDYMAN, MRS. ZSA ZSA GABOR

Bruce is underrated.

Everybody thinks he's a pushover but he's not. He's very strong, and smart. He just knows what battles to fight. Bruce will definitely put his foot down when he feels like he needs to. But he knows how emotional and dramatic we are, and he doesn't get worked up over every little thing. He's just, "Oh, here we go again." He knows that we'll be yelling at each other one second, and by the time he comes home from the golf course we'll be making a cake together!

He's just so easygoing. As long as he has a roof over his head and food to eat, he's fine. Whereas our mom always likes things a certain way. She likes to run the household and he's not threatened by it.

When we were younger, he was all about dirt-biking and four-wheeling and racing cars, and he had go-carts and airplanes. Khloé always hung out with him when she was a kid. Up at our house on Lake Tahoe he had jetskis and water skis and he'd go wind-sailing. He has a very daring side to him. He'll say, "Let's go bungee-jumping!" He's definitely done it all. If you said, "Well, I bet you haven't wrestled with alligators," no, he's done that, too.

He's very active and positive and he just goes all day. Every morning he used to wake us up and remind us, "It's not just another day. It's another day to excel!" He was always in a good mood. Though when he drove us to school he insisted on listening to talk radio and that really annoyed us.

He loves carpooling Kylie and Kendall to school every day now. He doesn't believe in nannies. Of course maybe you have to use one occasionally but he'd rather look after the kids himself or have one of us do it.

He's very down-to-earth and simple. He's very happy to drive the same car for twenty years. He wore these plastic Adidas flip-flop sandals for years and finally the top of them fell apart. So he just duct-taped them together. When our mom saw them she was horrified. "What the hell are on your feet?" she said.

"My sandals!" he replied. "I love these! I've had them five years."

"We're buying you new ones right now," she shot back.

They're truly opposites, Bruce and Mom. He's kind of a slob and she's like Mrs. Zsa Zsa Gabor, in fur coats to the floor wearing diamonds to breakfast!

MR. FIX-IT

Khloé: Bruce is so good at everything around the house. He can fix anything or build anything. My husband, Lamar, isn't. He can literally do none of it. I'm more a handyman than he is. If you ask Lamar to hang a picture, he'll say, "With what?" I'm like, "A hammer and a nail!" So I still have to call Bruce! You'd think if you get married you wouldn't have to call Bruce anymore.

DOUBLING UP

Kourtney: We had so much fun with Bruce's kids when we were young. He had three boys and a girl and we had three girls and a boy, so it was just perfect and we all got along really well.

Right after Bruce and Mom got married, we started going up to his house on Lake Tahoe. It was all brown and orange, very seventies, so immediately Mom started redecorating. All the kids bunked together.

My stepbrothers liked to make fun of Rob in his Mickey Mouse underwear. One day they were skipping rocks and they hit Rob in the head. It gave him a big gash but it was an accident.

Bruce used to go fishing and Kim would go with him. Bruce's daughter Casey and I were really good friends and we loved ganging up on Kim. One day Kim was on the dock fishing and we actually went out there with picket signs that we had made, and we marched around yelling, "Down with Kimberly! Don't kill worms!" We taunted her for being so mean even though I don't think you even kill worms when you fish—aren't they already dead?

After Casey and I watched that movie *City Slickers* together we didn't want to eat veal because in the movie they saved the baby cow. We just refused one night so Bruce grounded us and sent us to our bedrooms without dinner. But my mom snuck us a banana.

Finally they separated me and Casey.

WAX WORK

Kim: I remember being in my twenties and meeting some new friends. One time we were changing clothes, and I said, "Um, have you ever heard of a bikini wax? It's a must, you need it!" And they said, "What is that?" Are you kidding me? Your mom never taught you? I thought that all moms teach you these things. I mean, at the age of eleven, we were getting waxed. At least just the middle of our eyebrows, at home. And then at

thirteen we were getting bikini waxes at the salon. It's not like we'd go to get our hair done, but bikini waxes were important.

Khloé: I had to teach my friends about waxing because their moms never taught them. They would be shaving themselves. When I first started getting underarm hair Mom took me to get waxed. She taught me to never shave there. Waxing leaves everything cleaner and lasts longer. Not everyone waxes their arms or underarms—I get that. But your bikini, I believe, should always be waxed.

Kourtney: When I went to college, these friends of mine said they'd never had a bikini wax. I was like, seriously? It was unbelievable. I thought, we have to do something about this.

My mom was the original wax queen. She started waxing our eyebrows when we were super young, I think in the seventh grade. And she would do them so far apart that it was ridiculous. Whenever I look at my old pictures I'm like, what the hell was she doing? I look so ugly and my eyes look weird, because she made my eyebrows seem like they were ten miles apart.

So that's where our waxing started. My mom had a wax kit like the ones that they have in a salon. Then we would go to the salon for our bikinis.

HOW TO WAX YOURSELF

The absolute most important thing is to be careful. I said to Khloé once, "Let me do your upper lip." She didn't even need it, but I just felt like doing something. Then I burned her skin and she had like two scabs.

◖ Get a high-quality waxing kit; it is more expensive but you'll be less likely to burn yourself. The brand doesn't matter, but make sure you get the real kind that plugs into the wall, not the one you put in the microwave.

◖ Take a pain reliever about an hour before you wax.

◖ Blow on the wax before you put it on your skin. And it's always smart to test the skin on your wrist. Better a burn on your wrist than on your upper lip. Or worse.

◖ A little bit of ice will help with swelling or redness if you are going out soon after.

I started doing my own waxes at home, just thinking it was fun to do on my arms. And then in college I had this horrible waxing experience. I didn't have a car at the time, and this lady had a salon just across the street. I thought, well, anyone can do waxing. They always did a good job wherever I went in L.A. But I was so wrong.

First of all she wore those rubbery nursing gloves that are definitely not gentle on your skin. And then she made me watch her wax me! She had this handheld mirror and said, "Hold this down here." It was traumatizing.

So I bought myself a wax kit and started doing it myself, and doing my friends, if they had a boyfriend in town and needed a quick fix. I was the go-to wax person. I got to where I truly could do a bikini wax on myself in ten minutes.

But now I'm all about laser. I've retired my waxing kit.

SPOILED But Not Spoiled Brats

Some people think that when we were growing up we must have been little Beverly Hills brats whose parents gave them everything they wanted.

That is a total misconception. Of course our parents provided food and shelter and clothing. And they gave us a lot of nice things beyond that. Yes, each of us did get a car in high school.

But with the car we had to sign a contract saying we would keep up our grade average in school, that we'd wash the car once a week and take care of it

I remember this photo like it was yesterday, but I have no idea where we were or why we were there! I just remember all the laughing we did. I was fourteen, being a silly girl, as usual. I love to make people laugh! — *Khloé*

and pay for our own gas and we'd have to remember on our own when to change the oil. And if anything ever happened to our cars, too bad. Our parents wouldn't help us repair it and they sure wouldn't buy us a new one.

Most of our friends in high school had credit cards of their own. But not us. Our dad used to say, "Nothing in life is for free; you girls aren't going to get just whatever you want." So no credit cards. He did let us use his credit card but we still had to pay for our own stuff beyond the basics. Our parents wouldn't foot the bill for Gucci shoes or designer clothes. If we wanted to do any serious shopping, we had to come up with the cash.

Kim even went into debt with our dad once and had to pay him back *plus interest.* It was just a couple thousand dollars, but to us, that was a lot. And our mom and dad made it very clear that we would be totally cut off after we finished school. So we all learned early on if you want money, you have to earn it.

Around the house we were expected to do work, too. We always had housekeepers growing up but they weren't allowed to clean our rooms. We had to do it ourselves.

In other words, we may have been spoiled, but we weren't brats! We weren't stomping our feet saying, "Daddy, we need it *now!*" Our parents wanted to teach us responsibility, which you might not appreciate when you're a teenager. But now we're glad they did because it made us grateful for what we had and taught us a strong work ethic, which is so valuable in life.

IT'S IN MY CONTRACT

◀◀ KIM ▶▶

Our dad made us sign contracts for a lot of things. And he wasn't kidding about them, either. He had been an attorney, after all. I got into an accident right after I got my first car, a BMW. It was bumper-to-bumper traffic; I dropped something and bent down to pick it up and I rear-ended someone. So I had just turned sixteen and now my car was all messed up and I had to get it fixed myself. That's when I got my first job ever, at a clothing store in Encino, to pay for the repairs. I'd work there after school until 8 p.m., and I worked there a long time, until I started working at my dad's office.

MARYMOUNT HIGH SCHOOL
Los Angeles, CA
ID CARD ONLY
M H S
94 95
GRADE 9
ID. # 1105
KIMBERLY N. KARDASHIAN

CONTRACT

I, Kimberly Kardashian, in consideration of receiving a 1996 automobile from my wonderful and kind father, Robert, do hereby agree as follows:

1. All gasoline and repairs on the 1996 automobile shall be the responsibility of Kimberly. Kimberly shall receive a Standard Oil gasoline credit card in her own name and she shall be responsible for the payment of said gasoline credit card. Payments shall be made to Kimberly's father, Robert, on a monthly basis. In the event Kimberly fails to make said monthly payment to her father, Robert, Kimberly hereby agrees that she will be unable to drive her 1996 automobile until said bill is paid.

2. Part of Kimberly's duties and responsibilities are to drive her sister, Khloe' and her brother, Robert to their respective weekly activities. In addition, Kimberly shall run various errands for her father and help out whenever necessary. In the event Kimberly refuses or fails to drive her brother and sister to their respective activities or Kimberly refuses or fails to assist her wonderful father in any way, Kimberly's automobile shall be taken away for the upcoming weekend.

3. In the event Kimberly talks back to either her mother or father or refuses to obey either her mother or father, Kimberly agrees that her 1996 automobile may be taken away for an unspecified period of time, according to the discretion of either her mother or father.

4. Kimberly hereby acknowledges that her grade point average is over a 3.0 at Marymount High School. In the unlikely event that Kimberly's grade point average falls below 3.0 she agrees that she will not have the use of her 1996 automobile until her G.P.A. returns to 3.0 or better. This provision is absolute and cannot be changed or modified by either parent.

5. Kimberly agrees that she shall keep her car clean and neat at all times. Kimberly agrees that she shall wash her car once a week and shall cover her car at all times whenever her car is to be left outside all night long.

6. Kimberly agrees that in the very unlikely event that she takes drugs of any kind, smokes cigarettes or marijuana and or drinks alcohol excessively, then her car WILL be taken away for a period of six (6) months. This provision is irrevocable and cannot be modified by either parent. It is absolute.

7. Kimberly, your dad loves you very much and I am very pleased, happy and thrilled to give you your first new car. Enjoy and drive safely.

Executed this __25__ day of October, 1996.

Kimberly Noel Kardashian
Kimberly Noel Kardashian

Robert G. Kardashian

*KARDASHIONARY DEFINITION

KHLO-MONEY: A nickname for Khloé; also the name of her alter-ego during her teen years.

DERIVATION: Khloé: When I was sixteen I took myself out of regular school and enrolled myself in home-schooling at the Alexandria Academy. I never enjoyed class much and the hour-long commute seemed so far without my sisters. This place was pretty close to my dad's house. They'd give you classwork once a week and you could go at your own pace, so if you finished it ahead of time, you could go back and get more. I wanted to be done with it all, so I graduated when I was seventeen with a 3.8 grade point average. Not bad, right?

The rule in our house, though, was if you weren't getting a proper education, you had to work. So Kourtney didn't have to work because she was in college, but when I switched schools I had to get a job. I did all sorts of things here and there to earn money—babysitting, doing assistant things for friends. Nicole Richie gave me the nickname Khlo-Money (or Money for short) because I was supposedly the one in our crowd that always had money. She lived in Bel Air and all that but her parents were very restrictive with her spending. I didn't go around with wads of cash on me, but I did have cash.

BE-ATCH

Kourtney: It's true we weren't little divas, but I could be quite rude when I was younger, and I even took pleasure in it. One time we were getting ice cream and the lady who worked behind the counter was really mean to Kim. So I said something mean back to her. My dad got so mad at me. And then once at my dad's house, it was just him and me and Kim, and I said, "Everyone in this house is so fat except for me!" I was talking about Kim, of course, and she knew it. I was such a little bitch! I would say things on purpose, always the low blows, whatever would get under someone's skin. Sometimes I'm still a little bit like that, but only when someone really deserves it.

GALLOPING THROUGH LIFE

Khloé: I started riding horses when I was a kid and eventually I even got to have my own horse. Every day after school I went to a ranch off Sunset Boulevard out in Pacific Palisades near the ocean. I leased a horse then named Joey, a brown and white pinto. That was when I was eleven or twelve, and then a few years later I got my first horse, a black stallion named Guinness. He was wild, and would kick and throw me off. He really needed to be ridden every day. When you own a horse, it has to be treated like a job.

You have to take care of his stall and groom him and ride him. Eventually I realized I didn't have enough time to devote to him. My mother's friends always had horses, so I'd ride other people's horses instead. I helped Kendall learn to ride, too. She's good at it. I still ride when I can.

Kourtney learned to ride for *Filthy Rich: Cattle Drive*, a TV show she did, so near the end of her pregnancy when we took a trip to Santa Barbara, I thought we could all go out on horses one day. (Kim doesn't really ride, but she's okay just going for a trail ride on horseback.) I didn't realize riding horses is dangerous when you're pregnant. Kourtney had to stay behind.

When we were filming our second season in Miami, we went to polo practice and the players taught me how to play. It was hard at first, but then I had so much fun!

Our high school threw a father-daughter dance every year and we always had so much fun. I think Kim and I are both wearing vintage lingerie as dresses. It seemed super-cute then, but how fashion changes! — Kourtney

3
TEEN QUEENS

We don't know what "teen queens" really means but it sounded good. It is true we were popular and all that. But we weren't stuck up or ridiculously into ourselves.

When we entered seventh grade, we all went to all-girl Catholic schools. Khloé, too. We are Christian, not Catholic, but our parents thought we would get the best education there, and they liked that it was strict.

We had to wear uniforms, which we actually didn't mind. In fact, we liked it, because it made dressing for school really easy. And it put everyone on an equal level, so there wasn't a lot of competition with the way you dressed, though we did try to wear the coolest sneakers possible. We'd always add our own little touch, like keeping our pajama pants under our skirts, or wearing thermal long-sleeved shirts under our short-sleeve tops. For a while we wore boxers under our skirts. Who knows why we thought that was cool.

Some people think it might be weird not having boys around but it really wasn't. In a way, it made us more comfortable speaking up in class. You just didn't worry so much about how you looked or acted when there were no guys there, even though our parents had instilled confidence in us anyway.

We had lots of friends at other schools and met boys at parties on weekends. It seems like we went to a lot of bar mitzvahs and bat mitzvahs.

In those days we socialized mostly by talking on the phone, even with our supposed boyfriends. We would spend hours on the phone. But Dad would always make us hang up at a certain time and the phone would be off-limits for the rest of the night. It was like a phone curfew and it was always earlier than our friends'. But he used to tell us it was actually better for us that way. He'd say, "Trust me, if you have to get off the phone it makes guys want to talk to you more. If other girls talk all night, that makes them boring." And he was right! When you're a little less available it makes you more interesting.

We were popular and we had fun and all that, but we really weren't out very much, and our parents almost always knew what we were doing. The rule was we had to be home by eleven, and all our friends got to stay out much later. Our dad would try to say the same thing he did with the phone, you know, people will want to see you more if you have to go home earlier. But we'd sleep at our friends' houses and do other things to get around it.

If we did something wrong, our dad was the one we'd be worried about. Because he wouldn't just threaten to ground us or take away our car. He would definitely do it. We knew he was serious. With our mom, we knew we could usually talk our way out of it. Or maybe she'd ground us but then she'd let it go after a few days.

Mom was just more lenient. She would let us hang out with boys, but our dad wouldn't. He didn't want us being alone with guys at all. He always told us, "Never have sex until you're married!" We were his little girls and he didn't want us doing anything. He wanted us to be perfect.

MOM *WAS* JUST MORE LENIENT. SHE WOULD LET US HANG OUT WITH BOYS, BUT OUR DAD WOULDN'T.

KOURTNEY: Kim, remember the time when you were at tennis camp and you got caught kissing a boy? Dad got so mad, he was like, "Get in the car, we're going up there right now!"

KIM: He really tried to just yank me out of camp completely, but I think I got to stay in the end. That must have been when I was about twelve.

KOURTNEY: My friends and I at camp used to lie and say we'd kissed boys even though we hadn't, because everyone else was saying they had. I had my real first kiss in eighth grade, at a friend's house. The lights were off and everyone was kissing someone. It was so funny, like, okay, people, time to kiss!

KIM: We always used to hang out with him and his best friend, remember? So I think I was kissing the friend!

KOURTNEY: But the guy I kissed wasn't my boyfriend at the time. I actually had a boyfriend, you know, the kind of phone boyfriend that you mostly talked to but didn't see. He had bronchitis for like, two weeks, so I never saw him once while he was my boyfriend!

KIM: Yeah, and then you made me call him and pretend it was you and break up with him on his answering machine! We did everything together back then, had the same friends, double-dated.

KOURTNEY: We were both into long-term relationships in high school.

KIM: I dated T.J. (he was Michael Jackson's nephew) for five years. He was great, so considerate and sweet.

KOURTNEY: My first boyfriend turned out to be a jerk. He was athletic and good-looking and popular, but I eventually found out he was a cheater. He was from the Valley, and after we broke up for a long time I thought, "I hate everyone from the Valley!" Of course, I love the Valley. I live in the Valley!

VALLEY GIRL

Kourtney: In high school I lived with my dad mostly. At my mom's there were a million kids and it was chaos. At my dad's it was calm, and he was easygoing. In the morning I'd just grab a cup of cereal and eat it in the car while he drove me to school. He didn't care if I made my bed before I left. I wasn't a slob—my room was still clean—but my mom, if you didn't make your bed, she'd freak out.

Kim spent a lot of time there, too, and it was fun to invite friends over and lay out by the pool with music playing. Dad always knew what we were doing and knew all of our friends so he was fine with it. It was a good fit for me at that age.

BeinG a KardasHian
WASN'T SO GREAT

This was taken not long after I got married. I think I look fab if I do say so myself. A good Kodak moment for once! LOL! — *Khloé*

Khloé: Excuse me for butting into Kim and Kourtney's chapter, but I felt I should give you a slightly different perspective on the so-called Teen Queen years. The fabulous Kardashian sisters were not an easy act to follow.

When I was a kid (and for all my life, actually) I just didn't look like my sisters. When I was little I was cute and petite, and I had a big curly kind of afro. But then I got very chunky. After the divorce and during the O.J. trial when there was so much stress in the household, all everyone did was give us food, whatever we wanted, and my brother and I got to be fat little kids.

So from about the time I was nine or so I was chubby, and I had light, curly hair and light skin, and braces. I didn't feel pretty at all. It didn't help that Mom gave me this short haircut that just accentuated the roundness of my face. Whereas my sisters were these dark beauties and glamorous and tiny.

So then I had to go to the same school as theirs, where they were known as babes; everyone thought that to date one of the Kardashian girls was the ultimate. Everyone would say, "Oh my God, you're a Kardashian sister? You look nothing like them!" And it's true, I looked nothing like them. It's happened my entire life, but then it was the worst, with these two sisters who were drop-dead gorgeous. Once a guy I liked said to me, "Your sister is so hot!" I got a complex for a while after that and didn't want anyone to be around Kim or Kourtney. My self-esteem definitely suffered.

It was not fun to be their sister at that time.

Then at some point when I was a teenager I started working out. I went to Tae Bo with my mom, I rode horses. I lost weight and I got such great attention. Everyone from my mom's friends to my friends said, "You are so beautiful! You're so thin!" I just loved it. I'd never had that attention before. I had always been the chubby, "cute" one. I wanted the compliments to keep coming, so I just struggled to get thinner and thinner.

But at some point I went to the extreme. I wasn't anorexic or bulimic, thank God, but I guess I wasn't eating as much as I should have, and I started working out so much that I became incredibly thin. Sometimes I would go to the gym three times a day, and I had weights in my bedroom so I'd always be lifting. At my heaviest, I was probably a size 10 or 12. But during this time I got down to a size 0, which I can't even imagine now. Once when Kourtney came back from college we were working out together, and I fainted. She was so upset she was crying. She took me home and made me a bagel and cream cheese and said, "Eat this!" She was almost force-feeding me. "Okay, just eat more!"

My parents didn't realize what was happening. They just thought I was losing weight naturally because of puberty.

I remember the first time I ever saw someone who clearly had an eating disorder. We used to go out to visit our grandparents in Palm Springs, my dad's parents. They lived in a complex that had a pool for every six houses, that you shared. There was a mom there who looked anorexic, and it seemed like she'd made her teenage daughter anorexic, too. They looked very

K-TIP FROM KHLOÉ

WATCH YOUR MOUTH

You know how sometimes you go around saying, "Oh, I'm so fat," or "I feel so enormous" even if you're just bloated? Or "I'm so disgusting today!" At least I tend to. Well, if there are any little kids in the vicinity, just shut up! It's so much easier in life to believe the negative than it is to believe the positive—that's what my dad always said. And kids are so impressionable. So you should never say negative things like that around them, because they'll take it to heart and think, "Oh, that's fat?" and start stressing about themselves. And while you're at it, you might as well stop saying those nasty things about yourself altogether, and even thinking them, too, because it doesn't do you any good, either. Always try to stay positive, dolls!

unattractive and sad, sickly even, though I don't think they realized it. The only thing they drank was water, and they ate celery all day. At my NaNa's house, you always ate, and it was usually heavy stuff, delicious and hearty. My NaNa used to invite the daughter over to try to get her to eat but it never really worked.

It's very early on that kids can begin to feel pressured. You don't even have to say, "Oh, you're fat!" It was enough that I always got, "Why don't you look like your sisters?" And then when I got skinny it changed to, "Oh, you're so pretty!"

It's not like they intend to be hurtful or even realize what they're doing, but it's amazing how adults can do or say things that absolutely devastate you when you're young. I never thought I had a big nose growing up. But one day when I was about fourteen I went to lunch at La Scala restaurant in Beverly Hills with my mom and a friend of hers.

We were in a booth and I was eating my salad and the friend said to me, "You don't look Armenian at all!" My mom didn't say anything, but I could see her in the mirror. She pointed at her own nose and mouthed the words, "It's her nose!"

I thought, *What? Excuse me?* After that I always thought, *God, I have a huge nose!* And then I always wanted to get a nose job. (Oh, my mom wants me to tell you that she didn't know that I could see her in the mirror, which is true, but she definitely knows now because she says I've told her a thousand times.)

As I've gotten older, though, I think I've grown into my nose. And when I lost weight, my nose got smaller, too. A celebrity magazine did a photo shoot of me and my sisters once and when I saw it in the magazine, I said, "What have they done? That is not my nose!" The photographer had Photoshopped it to make it smaller, and I just didn't look like me. So that made me realize that I really don't want a nose job.

I remember my dad was taking me to elementary school one day and I said something like, "I wish I was as pretty as Kim." And he replied, "Kim might be beautiful but you have the personality." He never said I wasn't pretty or that Kim didn't have a personality. But it made me realize I had something going for me. I do have a great personality, and I know it takes me a long way.

I eventually learned to get over myself and stop feeling bad about being different from Kim and Kourtney. I mean, I always think I'm pretty now. I'm very confident. My sisters say, "How did you get all that confidence?" By going through what I did!

You just have to know your strengths in life. And if someone doesn't appreciate who you are or what you look like, that's their problem.

OH, AND ONE MORE THING, OR TWO

khloé: By the way, when those other two were living it up, I was cleaning up their messes. Literally. When Kourtney graduated from high school, she threw a party at Mom's house in Calabasas. People were smoking and drinking and the next morning Mom was furious. There were cigarette butts in all the flower pots and beer cans everywhere. I remember this very well because I had to clean it all up. I was Mom's total slave back then. You have no idea.

But I guess I liked having my sisters around sometimes. One time in the eighth grade these football players were talking trash about my dad, over the O.J. thing probably. I was upset and I went to tell Kourtney. So she went to my school, to the field where the football team was practicing, and told them, "You need to apologize to my sister or I will beat your asses!" And I couldn't believe it. They not only listened to my five-foot-tall sister—they obeyed!

4

DON'T TRY THIS AT HOME

by Khloé

I was a bad teenager.

That is *not* to say I was bad in the sense of doing drugs or drinking. I never ever did drugs and I didn't drink at all then either. But I would do bad things. You know that bedroom of mine with its own patio door? I would stuff my bed with pillows and sneak out through that door all the time when I was supposed to be asleep.

My mom taught me how to drive when I was thirteen, so if one of our baby sisters had an emergency I could drive to the hospital. But I took advantage of it. I used to steal her car or Bruce's, and I'd go over to this guy's house. He was a lot older than me, though he lied and said he was younger. Of course, I lied, too, and said I was sixteen. I was doing really well in school until I met him.

This guy was very, very manipulative, and I ended up losing my virginity to him when I was only fourteen. When my dad found out I was having sex he went ballistic.

I finally realized what an awful, bad person I was spending my precious time with. I really wasn't comfortable at all having sex with him in the first place. That was the first time I saw how easily older guys can take advantage of pretty young things who don't know any better. I stopped seeing him, and then I got back on the honor roll at school.

But it was a very rough way to learn my lesson. I was only fourteen but I thought I was so mature, and I look back and see how wrong I was. You should never, EVER have sex when you're that young. I always say that now. Having sex for the first time is an extremely important decision that affects your whole life. It should never be a "Come on, hurry up," thing, or an "Okay, I guess I might as well" thing and it *definitely* shouldn't be a "Well, he really wants me to so I guess I will" thing. Feeling rushed and pressured and unsure should have been my clue that I wasn't ready to take that step. I didn't really consider the consequences, or realize I should have been totally confident in what I was doing. Your first time should be a wonderful experience that you really appreciate, and that happens only when you take the time to wait until you know *for sure* it's right for you. Honestly, I promise you'll be so happy if you do.

And I *do* think you *shouldn't* be dating older guys at that age in the first place, because it's so likely to lead you where you really don't want to go.

I did other things I shouldn't have, too, when I was in my bad-girl phase. I was in this store once with Kim while she was shopping and she really liked these Dolce & Gabbana pants. So I stole them and tried to give them to her later. It was crazy! I don't know why I did all that stuff. Maybe because I wanted to be different from my sisters, or get attention. I don't know.

I was just very rebellious at that age, and I started hanging out with a much older crowd. I went to my first club with Paris Hilton when I was fourteen. She put a red wig on me and told me, "Say you're a *Playboy* centerfold." And I swear, I didn't

Kourtney

Dear Khloé,
what's up? How is the grounded life treating you? I hope it is fun and exciting! I was just thinking about my little (big) Khlo-ball and so I thought I would write you a note. I also wanted to ask you if you would be my Valentine - please!?! I love you and miss you!
♥Kourtney

even know what that meant. She had me hold a cigarette that wasn't lit. I just had to hold it, because she said it would make me look older. So people kept saying, "What do you do?" And I'd say, "I'm a *Playboy* centerfold!"

I stayed a lot at this house owned by a celebrity whose name we shall not mention. A lot of his friends and people who worked for him stayed there, and sometimes I did errands for them. They were really nice to me, but the bottom line was that they were older than me, and involved in stuff that I shouldn't have been around.

One night I had a bad experience with one of the people hanging out at this house, this guy with a violent temper who was really scary. Without

I like to do fun things for my husband, and we're both very silly people. I try to be creative, so because Lamar is *totally* addicted to candy, I thought that posing for him this way would be double the pleasure! — *Khloé*

going into every little horrible detail, I almost had something really, seriously bad happen to me. I mean, I was frightened and a little bit hurt, but it could have been much, much worse.

Once I got out of there alive, I decided to never talk to those people again and cut them out of my life completely. At least that's what I told myself I was going to do. But apparently I hadn't yet come to my senses about the whole situation.

It was probably only a week after that I got a call from one of the people from the house who'd been friendly with the sicko freak. He wanted me to come over so they could apologize. He sounded really sorry, so I got in my car to drive there.

But on the way over, I got into a major car accident and went through the windshield. (My seat belt was on but it was under my shoulder instead of over. Really smart.)

They had to saw the car apart to get me out. It was totaled, of course, my poor little Mercedes C-class. I remember my father said to me at the hospital, "You sure look better than your car!" My face wasn't really banged up—it was the top of my head that broke the glass—but I had a concussion and my knees were really messed up. I had to have two surgeries on one knee and I have only artificial cartilage in it now.

When Kim got there I thought she was my mom. At least that's what she says. I don't remember. I still can't remember everything that happened around that time. It's very fuzzy in my head.

I had to stay in bed for three weeks and I couldn't do anything. My best friend Malika and her twin sister Khadijah washed my hair for me. I had a brace from my pelvis to my ankle and I had to be on crutches for three months.

But once again, I actually was very lucky, because I could have been in a coma or paralyzed, or worse. Lying around stuck in one spot like that gave me a lot of time to reflect on my life. By the time I was physically healed, I just had no desire to be around those people anymore. I knew they weren't good for me.

All of which explains why I believe that everything happens for a reason. I should never have been hanging out with those guys. I'd barely escaped from those people with my life and yet I was still going back to that house! I had been moving at such a fast pace in my life, way too fast. That accident was like God literally stopping me in my tracks, saying, "Slow down and wake up!"

This all happened when I was sixteen or seventeen. So you know, I kind of grew up quickly. I went through a lot when I was very young. Thank God I wasn't drinking on top of all my bad-girl behavior, because I would probably still be on a downhill slide today.

I don't regret what happened, because it's made me the way I am. But I don't think most people could handle it. I definitely wouldn't recommend it to anyone else!

Amen, sistahs!

Khloé— 2001

Happy Birthday, doll! I wish that I could be there to celebrate with you, but I will be home in 2 days and Forever may you reign.

Happy Birthday

We will celebrate on Saturday! Here is a cool paper with your name on it, just incase you forget what it is. (Now you know how bored I am here in good ol' Tucson... yee-haw!) I love and miss you cutie munch, sweat apple tart, honey dew melon with cool whip, chilli cheese frie and plum diddle, you! ♥, Kourtney

WHEELS

Kourtney: After I totaled my first car, a black 3 series BMW, my parents made me get a Toyota 4Runner, a mid-sized SUV, because they thought it would be safe. When I got back from college, I bought Kim's car, a white BMW, with money from my savings. But after a while it was getting old; the car window on the driver's side wouldn't roll down, so if I was going to a drive-through I'd have to open the door to get the food. So I made an appointment with my dad at his office, and I presented my case. I'd found a great car that wasn't too expensive and I asked if he'd buy it for me. He said, "Nope. You have to buy it yourself." Even though I hated it at the time, I was so happy on the day I finally got it, all by myself. It was a Mercedes CLK, silver with a black interior, and I loved it. Later on when I went into a sports car phase I used to drive a Maserati. It was the worst car, such a rough ride and so unreliable. I'd get flat tires all the time.

Then when I got pregnant with Mason, I decided I wanted the perfect Mommy car that would be completely safe and dependable. I was going to get an SUV but I'm so glad I didn't. It's hard enough getting into an SUV myself because I'm so short, but then lifting a baby into one would just be too much. Instead I got a Mercedes 550S, black with a black interior, and I love it. Literally, it's the smoothest ride ever.

MY FAVORITE CAR EVER IS . . .

KHLOÉ: my Range Rover

KIM: my black Bentley

KOURTNEY: my Mercedes S550

THE CAR I WRECKED WAS . . .

KHLOÉ: my Mercedes C Class

KIM: my first car, a BMW

KOURTNEY: my first car, a BMW

MY CAR HAS TO HAVE . . .

KHLOÉ: tinted windows and navigation

KIM: a reverse camera

KOURTNEY: a smooth ride— and black interior

Kim: My first white Range Rover was so special. It was the first car I got on my own. It had pink trim and it was such a smooth ride, so comfortable to be in, and luxurious. Now I have a black Range Rover and a black Bentley. Range Rovers ride the best. I'm a total neat freak and my car is no exception. In fact, my Range Rover is so dirty right now it's driving me crazy! I've got to get it washed immediately!

Khloé: First I had a black Tahoe, then a Mercedes C-class, and a small Hummer after that. Right now I have two Range Rovers, actually. One is gray with a black interior and millions of Swarovski crystals. I wanted a newer one, though, so now I have one that's white with a black interior. Rob has been driving the gray one and he's like, "Can't we get rid of those rhinestones?" And I'm like, "Do you know how much it cost to put those in?"

OCD in the DNA

Khloé: I have a clean problem. If I'm not working, I feel like I have to be cleaning. I love everything really clean and organized. In my bathroom and in my refrigerator, everything's lined up and I have all the labels facing outward. My dad was like that. He had a walk-in closet that was perfectly organized.

Lamar is sloppy and leaves things all over the floor, but he's been in the NBA for ten years so he's used to being at hotels and having people pick up after him all the time.

I hate folding laundry. It's really tedious because I'm so OCD about it, and it takes me much longer than the average person. But I'm really good at cleaning, because I'm very efficient and meticulous. I'm the world's best bed maker. Kim actually offered once to pay me to be her housekeeper.

Kim's neat like I am. But Kourtney's house, what a mess. When I lived with her it was a nightmare. I could just never feel like it was clean even in my room. Kourtney is a slob, even though she's an organized slob.

Kim: I am a huge neat freak, and a bit of a control freak, too. I'm just super organized. I'm, like, neater than my house-keeper. I got it from my dad. My brother Rob is even more organized than me!

Every morning I get up and make my bed, and I can't leave the house if my place is a mess. Or if anyone's stuff is messy. I just wouldn't be able to have a normal day. I don't like vacuuming or mopping or taking the trash out, but laundry is perfect for me. I worked in a clothing store so I definitely know how to fold. I'm very good at folding.

My scrapbooks and photo albums are catalogued by date. Everything in my purse is organized in separate compart-ments. Nothing is just thrown in there. I know where every single thing is in my closet, exactly. I hate it when a guy, you know, you've just finished straightening the closet and he starts taking out every other shirt and ruining it. I have all black velvet hangers. If I ever saw another kind of hanger in my wardrobe, I'd die.

Whenever I'd sleep over at a friend's house in high school, I'd go through their stuff and say, "You're such a slob! You need to have everything organized!" I would stay up organizing their entire closet. We had so much fun.

Kourtney says she's organized, but she's got piles everywhere. She knows what each pile is and what's in it and where it's going, but it's such an unorganized bunch of piles.

Kourtney:
Kim and Khloé say that I'm a slob, but I'm a major organizer. I'm weirdly obsessed with everything being orderly. There are piles everywhere in my house and my sisters find that annoying, but it's because I don't do something unless it's done perfectly. Like I cleaned up my closet the other day and then I had bags of stuff. And for each one, I have something to do, like this one goes to shoe repair, and I have to take that one for alterations, like that.

But in my drawers everything has a place. I have drawers of tank tops and T-shirts folded and grouped according to black, whites, neutrals, and colors. In the kitchen, my dishes are perfect, and the glasses are all lined up. My refrigerator is perfect. And I do have to have some things a certain way. Like I only want pink dish gloves.

My dad was very organized. His closet was totally orderly, with hangers all the same. Scott is not like that at all. He leaves his clothes on the floor. He says he loves clothes, but then why wouldn't you have your suits on good hangers and lined up in a row according to colors? I just don't get it. Trust me, I've been to his place in New York and there's nothing organized about it. I used to go into the kitchen while he was still sleeping and start throwing things away without him knowing. I would take out trash bags full of gross stuff that had been forgotten in drawers for ten years. Mason will definitely know better.

KIM AND KHLOÉ SAY THAT I'M A SLOB, BUT I'M A MAJOR ORGANIZER. I'M WEIRDLY OBSESSED WITH EVERYTHING BEING ORDERLY.

5

ESCAPE FROM BEVERLY HILLS

by Kourtney

I always wanted to go to college. It was a miserable experience at first—but then it was fab!

I was originally planning to go to the University of Arizona in Tucson. I knew so many people who were going there that it was almost like UA was an extension of Beverly Hills. My boyfriend at the time was going there, too, and friends of mine kept saying, "Don't follow him, go do your own thing!" I pretty much ignored them.

One time it was taco night at our good friends' house and I had this big conversation with my dad and his friend there. They were also into the idea of me going away and doing my own thing. They asked, why go to the same school as everyone else I knew? Why not go off to explore and have new adventures? They thought I would get more out of college if it wasn't just a continuation of the whole social scene I already knew from high school.

My dad especially thought it would be good for me to have my independence in a different environment. He didn't come out and say he didn't want me hanging on my boyfriend's arm, but I know he didn't want me to get too attached and miss out on a lot of experiences. He liked Dallas. It was a big city, whereas Tucson was a smaller kind of place. Everyone from L.A. who went to Tucson would just fly home every weekend on Southwest. He made it sound exciting to leave my comfort zone and try something new. He convinced me to do my own thing, so I changed my mind at the last second and went to SMU, Southern Methodist University in Dallas, Texas.

It didn't seem like such a good idea, though, when I first got there. My dad came with me to help move me in and we were both crying. It was so sad. I kept saying, "Don't make me stay!"

Because I made my choice so late, the only place for me to live was in an upperclassman dorm. It was so odd. It turns out that upperclassmen don't really stay in the dorm much. My roommate had a boyfriend and she was never there. All my friends were across campus in other dorms. I was basically alone. I went from being with all my sisters and my brother and my mom and dad and Bruce to . . . just me. I was so homesick. I would call my dad and cry every day and beg him, "Please don't make me stay here." He wrote me the sweetest letter. I wish I still had it but my box full of old letters and things like that got moldy and I had to throw it away. :(

I remember my mom and Khloé came to visit me and the last night we were leaving a restaurant and I was crying and pleading, "Please don't leave without me!"

After the first semester, my dad told the school, "If you don't switch her dorm I'm taking her out of the school." So I moved to the dorms where my friends lived. And that made a huge difference!

> I REMEMBER MY MOM AND KHLOÉ CAME TO VISIT ME AND THE LAST NIGHT WE WERE LEAVING A RESTAURANT AND I WAS CRYING AND PLEADING, "PLEASE DON'T LEAVE WITHOUT ME!"

At the time, I was used to Beverly Hills, and the people at SMU were so different from the people I knew back home. I know some people think of women in Dallas as blondes with big hair, decked out to the nines. But it wasn't like that. The people there were Southern, or from other parts of the country, and they didn't care about what you wore, or who you knew, or how much money you had. They were sincere and down-to-earth, without the cattiness that's so much a part of L.A. And they were really fun. We could have fun just going to Blockbuster and making cupcakes and watching movies.

I also felt it was the first time I was really making my own friends, not just friends that were kids of my mom's friends, people I was hanging out with since I was about two years old. At college, people didn't know me from that life, no one knew my family. So it was kind of cool.

The whole thing was a great learning experience. Even the way I got around. In L.A., you never walk anywhere. Really, never. But in Dallas my first year I didn't have a car, so I walked all over. I learned how to do my own laundry, and I went out to eat by myself. I relied on myself more than I ever had before. It made me realize I was okay on my own. And if I was homesick I would go to this little

SEPARATION ANXIETY

◄◄ KIM ►►

When Kourtney went to college I was devastated, just heartbroken. I cried hysterically. And she didn't go local, like Arizona where everyone else went. It was far away. I was nervous for her, and we would talk on the phone every day. It was a good experience for her and I'm glad she went but it was just weird for her to be away. She made me move in full time with my dad so he wouldn't be alone. When Kourtney and I were apart for that time it was probably my first push toward independence.

outdoor shopping center about a mile from SMU full of high-end stores . . . Prada, Chanel, Ralph Lauren. I'd get Starbucks and window shop. I felt like a mix of Audrey Hepburn in *Breakfast at Tiffany's* and Cher from *Clueless*.

My dad was right. He knew being on my own would be so much more enriching. I am so glad that I went away and got to have that experience.

For my second year, my dad and I drove all the way from L.A. to Dallas. The drive to Dallas was the trip of a lifetime. *ROAD TRIP!* My dad and I had an absolute blast. I was driving my mom's series BMW that she had given me . . . it was a fabulous car, but *no* CD player! We listened to local radio stations in every town we drove through. We drove through the middle of nowhere to get to Dallas, and had a ball.

That year I was in an apartment with my friends and we had a great time. I talked a lot with my friends in Arizona, though, and for junior year I decided to transfer. By then my friends knew a lot of people from the East Coast and all over and I got to be friends with their friends.

I was studying communications and journalism, and Spanish was my minor. But the last year I changed my major, so I had to stay an extra semester. I changed to theater arts because I wanted to study costume design. I had taken a fashion design class in high school, and I used to make outfits for my friends when we'd go out. In college I always liked to do something creative, like buy plain tank tops and decorate them.

For my major I had to take stagecraft. And lighting design, which I just didn't get. For our final project we had to light a body form called *Miss New York* and I had no idea what to do. So I would just grab any color fabrics and stick 'em in the lights, and then you had to go to the lighting board and move things up and down. Everyone was doing deep, slow music as background and moving the lights slowly but I chose a Madonna song and I was like a DJ with the lights, moving them all around really fast. I didn't know what I was doing but the instructor loved it.

I also had to take acting courses, and I would get so nervous and embarrassed in front of the class that I would pretend to be sick almost every day. Improv was just terrifying. I know it's ironic, because now I'm on camera constantly for the shows and I could care less!

> I ALSO HAD TO TAKE ACTING COURSES, AND I WOULD GET SO NERVOUS AND EMBARRASSED IN FRONT OF THE CLASS THAT I WOULD PRETEND TO BE SICK ALMOST EVERY DAY.

BIGGEST FIGHT, EVER.

KHLOÉ: Back to the three of us now. Is this getting confusing? Follow along, girls! So remember the *Keeping Up* episode about Kim buying her Bentley? And Kourtney and I had this humongous fight with Kim? That was really terrible. Not talking to one another for five days is major for us. But if you think that was bad, once Kim and Kourtney had such a huge fight that they didn't speak for four months.

KIM: It was more like three.

KHLOÉ: Whatever. Maybe you already know—or maybe you don't— but Kim got married when she was nineteen.

KIM: I was really young and naive.

KHLOÉ: She was dating this music producer, really flashy. I'm sure it was very exciting for Kim. He was ten years older than you, right?

KIM: Something like that.

KHLOÉ: They eloped and got married in Vegas. And she didn't tell any of us in the family. No one knew! It was amazing.

KOURTNEY: But Kim was so naive if she wanted it to be a secret. We had a ton of the same friends and one of them told me, "I can't believe your sister just got married."

KHLOÉ: And random people were saying, "Congratulations, Kim got married!" I told her, "Oh no, it's just a joke."

KOURTNEY: But I was hinting to my mom, "Well, if people are saying something to you, maybe it's true." Because I knew it was true.

KHLOÉ: Kim denied it, though. She tried to tell our parents that Kourtney was lying, like, "She's just a college drunk, don't listen to her!"

KIM: Then Kourtney found my marriage certificate on the Internet.

KHLOÉ: If you get married in Vegas it's public record. And Kourtney knew that and found it online and told on Kim.

KOURTNEY: I e-mailed it to my mom and sent her the link.

KHLOÉ: I remember my dad picked me up from school the day he found out and he was livid, just like out-of-his-mind mad.

KIM: I told Kourtney, "You're ruining my life!"

KOURTNEY: So Kim and I didn't talk for months.

KHLOÉ: I was really protective of my sisters in general and Kim and I were really close at that time. I was just happy for Kim. So I was on her side.

KOURTNEY: Finally our dad made us talk to each other again.

KIM: That was definitely the longest time any of us ever were in a fight. Nothing since has come close.

I WAS REALLY PROTECTIVE OF MY SISTERS IN GENERAL AND KIM AND I WERE REALLY CLOSE AT THAT TIME. I WAS JUST HAPPY FOR KIM. SO I WAS ON HER SIDE.

In 2009 we opened a branch of Dash in Miami Beach.
— Kourtney, Kim, and Khloé.

6

WORK
IT

KOURTNEY: We didn't have to work when we were in school, but after college I was completely cut off.

KIM: I worked for our dad for a long time. He owned a company called MovieTunes that supplied all the music you listen to in the theater while you're waiting for the movie to start. We'd burn thousands of CDs all day and then send them out.

KHLOÉ: I worked there, too, after Kim, for two or three years. It was mostly secretarial duties at first, answering phones and stuff, but then there were more responsibilities. Our dad would always say, "When you come through these doors, I'm your boss." In other words, we had to kind of forget that we were his daughters in the work environment and not expect some kind of special treatment. Especially because other people at the office will be watching the boss's daughter.

KIM: It taught us not to take advantage of our positions. And it was a good lesson for us later on when we became bosses ourselves. He showed us that if you're in a business situation with people you know personally, you can be businesslike with them. In fact, it's better for everyone if you are.

KHLOÉ: I used to work as an assistant to different people. My job was looking after schedules and making sure things got done. One of my responsibilities was throwing parties. Sometimes I'd have only one day to cover her swimming pool and put together a party for one hundred people. I got to be pretty good at knowing how to make things happen.

KOURTNEY: And then tell about when those people told you a monkey could do your job better than you.

KHLOÉ: Can you imagine saying that to someone? They begged me to take that job in the first place and I didn't really want to. Then I finally said yes, because they needed the help so much. And then they're that rude to me? I eventually left but first I helped them find someone to replace me, which they didn't deserve.

KOURTNEY: That's a good lesson in how not to talk to your employees. You don't have to baby them but you should always treat them with respect.

KHLOÉ: Malika helps me out doing assistant things when she's between acting jobs. Because she's my best friend, at first I had a hard time telling her to do things so I'd baby-talk her. "Could you, um, pretty please do this?" Finally I told her it wasn't working out because I just couldn't give her orders like a regular boss. And she said, "That's your problem, not mine! I never told you to treat me differently." So now I've learned I don't have to fluff it all up when I tell her boss things.

KOURTNEY: Kim, you had so much stuff going on I couldn't keep up with you.

KIM: I started a business organizing closets. I got the idea from doing my friends' closets. And that led to selling lots of things on eBay for people. And then I became a stylist. I always knew I loved fashion and wanted to be in the business somehow. So sometimes I would style my friends, just to get my feet wet. And then I became a professional stylist almost by accident.

Our mom was doing infomercials and she was going to wear all these hideous outfits. I said, "Mom, let me get you some decent things to wear." So I styled one of her shoots for a fitness equipment company and got her great workout clothes. Then for Mom's next infomercial she needed interview-type clothes, so I dressed her in a fabulous suit. I just found it so easy. Mom looked great so the company hired me to do other infomercials. I also did it for a few celebs. And I learned a lot about dressing myself, too, like how to make the most of your good features and take the attention off your not-so-great ones. For example, I wear a lot of belts to accentuate my curviness. Also little tricks, like double-sided tape is a must for keeping your bra straps in place or making sure your neckline doesn't show too much cleavage. And certain colors, even particular shades of certain colors, will look better on you than others. Black will slenderize the parts of your body you want to look smaller, but it's good to have some contrast and splashes of color, especially if you're being photographed. You have to find out what brings out your skin tone. For example, whites and creams tend to look good with my skin because it's olive.

KOURTNEY:
After college I had a clothing line for a year that I did with a friend of mine. We did T-shirts at first and we did pretty well. We got into some cute little boutiques like Kitson. And remember, you guys, how I got an order from Nordstrom's, but my sales rep misunderstood and messed it up? So it never happened.

We didn't open Dash, our store in Calabasas, until later, so we'll wait to tell you all about that.

KHLOÉ:
Stay tuned, dolls!

My very first day at the Miami radio station. I was soooo nervous. I literally thought I would throw up on the air. I can still feel those emotions. – *Khloé*

RADIO STAR
◀◀ KHLOÉ ▶▶

When I went to Miami and started doing my show *Khloé After Dark*, I had no idea what I was doing. I had done radio spots before but I had never done a whole show, or directed one or hosted one. I'd never practiced before, or done all the preparation. Answering questions is a lot easier than coming up with them!

The first time I was nauseous. Just terrified. I wanted to call it off before it started. But then once I did it, it was actually fun, and people said I was a natural. I still have problems in one area: cutting people off. I'm very appreciative of people who call in and want to talk and I just hate to cut them off!

I can imagine doing radio as a real full-time job, maybe when I'm older.

73

BUY AND SELL

Kim: I'm a shopaholic. When I was eighteen I started getting really into eBay. You know, I'd buy things and then when I was over them I'd put them up on eBay. And I started doing it for my friends, too, especially after I'd clean out their closets for them. I felt like eBay was no trouble at all. When I was working at my dad's office, once a week I would bring a bag of stuff in, and I had my mannequin there, and after all my work was done I'd shut the door and photograph all the stuff and put them up on eBay. I'd spend half the day doing that. He didn't mind.

EBay is still one of my favorite things to do. I'm in love with the whole process—you can find anything you want from all around the world. I buy makeup that's been discontinued, vintage purses, and rare shoes you can't get anymore. I was always on a budget—I still am!—so I had a rule: If I want to buy something I have to sell something first. I sell mostly clothes and shoes and bags but I've sold other things, too. I sold Bruce's motorcycle for him.

I still do auctions once a month, though now I have people help me. And I'd say I'm still a shopaholic.

K-TIP FROM KIM

eBAY IT

If you become comfortable with the process and get a routine down, selling things on eBay is a good way to get rid of things you don't want anymore and make a little extra cash. It isn't hard but it does take effort and time.

◀ First set up a seller's account on eBay. It's not difficult.

◀ When you post an item, you have to upload a photo of what you're selling. Sometimes people don't, but it's much harder to get buyers interested in your stuff that way. With clothes, photographs are an absolute must. A regular digital camera works fine.

◀ Nothing beats a mannequin for showing off clothes. If you don't have one, then make sure you photograph your item against a plain background, light in color. That's very important. I used to sit on the floor of my bedroom with a pair of shoes on the floor in front of the white wall and take pictures from all angles.

◀ It helps to write a description of the item that sounds enticing. You want to make those potential buyers crave what you've got!

◀ Expect people to ask a ton of questions, and make sure you answer each and every one. And you need to check in frequently to make sure your responses are prompt. Being responsive will encourage people to buy. It can be time-consuming, but hey, it's profit we're talking about!

◀ Once you have a buyer, make sure you follow all the protocols set up by eBay and PayPal, if you're using it, to ensure you're protected.

◀ After you've sold an item, don't delay sending it to the buyer. You don't want anything to affect your rating as a seller; mine was always very high. But do take your time making sure you pack everything up properly and tape it just right. You'll also need to have the right labels and the right postage. EBay has a lot of information on their site that can help you with this part of it and in fact the entire process of selling, so take advantage of it!

◀ Try to concentrate on being a seller, not a buyer. Not that you won't want to buy things sometimes, but it's easy to get swept away shopping on eBay. Remember my rule: If I buy, I have to sell!

K-TIP FROM KHLOÉ

HOW TO THROW A SICK PARTY

◖ First write down everything you need, from food to dishes to tablecloths.

◖ Food and music are the key. If you've got good food and music, you don't even need chairs. I never play rap unless it's very pop kind of rap.

◖ Get flowers and candles and all but make sure the colors you use to decorate are cohesive and inviting. For example, the suite where we film in Miami is all different colors, which is good on camera, but in person, it's not easy on the eyes.

ShOP GIRLS

Kourtney: People probably associate us most with our women's clothing store, Dash, but Smooch actually came first.

At some point I was kind of over the T-shirt line I was doing. My partner and I had been butting heads and after my dad died I was reevaluating things, thinking, what do I want to do?

Our grandma MJ has always been a very chic woman, with little matching purses and all. Really classy and put together, even if she's in sweats. For thirty years, she owned a children's clothing store in La Jolla (near San Diego). Kim and I used to go down and visit on weekends and we'd help her in the store. Our mom always liked to dress the two of us in matching outfits, and they all came from there.

So one day Mom said, "I'm going to open a store! I've always wanted to do it and it would be so fun!" She asked me to be her partner. So I told Mom yes, and we started up a kids' clothing store called Smooch right in Calabasas.

We would go downtown together and I would do all the buying, selecting, and ordering of the merchandise. And my mom did the cutest windows! The two of us were always at the store, just us, because no one worked for us then.

Most of the customers knew us. Although sometimes people who didn't know us would assume I was just a sales clerk and would give me attitude. You know, treat me like a shop girl. They'd ask, "Who's the owner of the store?" I'd say "Me," and then they'd insist, "No, don't you mean your mother owns it?" And I'm thinking, I pay every bill, I do every check, I do everything! I've always looked younger than I am.

It was really fun. And focusing on Smooch helped me deal with my dad's death.

I threw myself into the store. I came early and left two hours after closing, every day. It became my baby and my obsession and I really put my emotion and time into it.

As I started getting busier with expanding Dash to Miami, being a new mom, and all the other projects that I was working on, it seemed time to

> IT *WAS* REALLY FUN. AND FOCUSING ON SMOOCH HELPED ME DEAL WITH MY DAD'S DEATH.

close Smooch. This was such a hard decision, but the store just wasn't the same without my mom and me there. I could no longer devote the time needed to keep the store as charming and fabulous as it once was. Seems odd timing, just after having a baby, I close my children's store. I miss it and know I will have a children's store again one day. And of course, we have Dash in L.A.

A couple years after we started Smooch, I decided I wanted to open another store. I asked Khloé if she wanted to do it with me and she said yes. And then Kim was like, "What about me?" She was mad that we hadn't included her, so the three of us opened Dash together.

We had the best time going to New York on buying trips for the store. We'd set up appointments and go to the fashion shows and order all the clothes. We'd treat ourselves and stay at nice hotels and restaurants and go out.

Now I mostly look at merch online and I'll consult with Kim and Khloé about what we want to order. We haven't taken one of our Dash trips to New York in . . . forever. Maybe someday when things aren't so crazy!

Kim: When Kourtney and Khloé decided to open a store by themselves, it was such a blow to me. I was a stylist and it would have been a dream come true for me to open a store. I was really offended and said, "What about me?" I guess they thought I wouldn't want to devote the time to it, but they didn't even ask. Finally they invited me to be a part of it and we all did it together.

It was like our baby. We had fun with it. We all worked in different roles. Kourtney definitely opened the business and handled the business side of it. I was more of a personal shopper. Sometimes my friends and I would order pizza at midnight and shop in private.

We're still very involved with Dash, but these days it's hard for us to even walk in the store without attracting too much attention to get our work done.

Khloé: When we first decided to open the store, I didn't think to include Kim because she was off doing her own thing. We wanted it to be our main focus, and knew it wouldn't be for her. Like right, I could see Kim working in the store. But she got really pissed so we invited her.

Kourtney had a vision for the store and she was on a mission. She had Bruce over there every single day painting, spackling, building crown moldings. He even built the dressing rooms. He did literally everything. I didn't want to be there while all this was going on but every day Kourtney would call me up, "Okay, so are you running over to come help us paint?"

At first it was just me running Dash, and Kourtney running Smooch. If Kourtney went to get lunch she'd get mine, too, and I'd watch Smooch while she was gone. And vice versa. We didn't have any employees for years, and we did everything ourselves. We cleaned the store, steamed the clothes, did the tagging and the inventory. And we had a ball. It was a nice, mellow, simple thing. We'd call each other in the morning before work and say, "Want a Starbucks?" And then we'd be at work all day long, and at the end of the day we'd say, "Wanna go to dinner?"

Kourtney still goes into the store sometimes, but I'm never there. I'm not needed anymore and I can make more money outside the store.

K-TIP FROM ALL OF US   SPEAK UP

Sometimes it's hard for girls, or even grown women, to be direct and simply say outright what they need to say. Maybe they're afraid of looking too full of themselves or don't want to offend anyone or think maybe they don't know what they're talking about. But some people don't seem to have any problem saying what they want to say. And neither should you. You don't have to be a bitch, but being direct doesn't make you a bitch.

We had close-up shots like this with our dad in frames all around the house. I was fifteen in this one. — Kim

ROBERT GEORGE KARDASHIAN

ur dad meant so much to us. He was really a big influence on us all and still is, to this day. When we were little we called him Dad when we talked to him, but whenever we were talking *about* him, we called him Daddy.

Our dad tried very hard to instill family values in us, and he succeeded! He used to say "Blood is thicker than water," and now we know what he meant. We are so glad we have such a strong bond with all of our family. We're there for each other no matter what.

Another thing our dad used to say was, "Money isn't happiness." He would point out certain people and say, "Look at all the money they have. And yet they're not happy!" Or he'd show us that they had a lot of money but they weren't very good people. He would take us to see homeless people living in cardboard boxes, to teach us compassion and make us realize how blessed we were. But at the same time, he taught us that our material blessings weren't the most important things in life.

81

He made us understand that the most important thing was to be a good person. Our dad never talked down to people, no matter who they were or what they did for a living. He always treated people with respect.

He gave us such a strong work ethic and made sure we never took anything for granted.

Dad made us feel so loved, and set such high standards for us. Without his influence in our lives, we can't even imagine what they'd be like today.

When he got esophageal cancer it was one of the worst times in our lives. They found it when it was already Stage 4, and had spread to his liver. He didn't have much chance of survival. But he didn't tell us all of that; he could barely talk but he didn't want us to worry. We all tried to have a positive attitude for him. Kourtney spent a lot of evenings with him watching old black and white movies. The very last one was *The Postman Always Rings Twice*. Once she made him a quesadilla and they talked about life. He was most concerned that Rob, who was only sixteen, finish high school and go to U.S.C.

He got really sick very quickly after that, though. He started losing a lot of weight and his muscles deteriorated. It wasn't long before he was on morphine, and he started throwing up profusely. It was so hard to be around him and see him suffering. In better times at his house, Kim used to make him cream of wheat, and that was all he wanted to eat at the end.

Only eight weeks after his diagnosis, he passed.

Our mom took us shopping. That may sound weird, but she always wanted us to look our best, and so we went to buy clothes for the funeral. She knew it was good to get us out of the house and do something together that would distract us for a while. And Kim wrote her funeral speech. She was so nervous but wanted to make our dad proud.

You know, everyone thinks that we're big trust fund babies, that we inherited a huge fortune from our dad, but it's not true. Six weeks before his death he got married, and almost everything of his went to his new wife. We did get a few personal things that we truly treasure, such as his Bible, which Kim has. And Rob got to keep his college fund, which made us all happy. Our dad got just what he wanted: Not only did Rob graduate high school, he went on to graduate from U.S.C.

YOU KNOW, EVERYONE THINKS THAT WE'RE BIG TRUST FUND BABIES, THAT WE INHERITED A HUGE FORTUNE FROM OUR DAD, BUT IT'S NOT TRUE.

because you're my #1 valentine!

I love you

Kimberly

aka

Jouge

Feb. 14 1998

Dad-

THAT'S WHY YOU HAVE ME !

I love being your roommate and better yet since we are both single right now I love being your valentine! I hope you have a great Valentine's Day. I love you even though lately I have been the "mean" sister & have had an attitude! I'm sorry (maybe it's the dateless Valentine's Day) well not really

My dad looks sooo handsome here! He was always a very dapper dresser. Rob looked handsome, too. I believe he was five and I was eight. — *Khloé*

This was a card to my dad when I was living with him in high school. He always called me "Jouge." We would laugh because no one knows where it came from! — *Kim*

MERRY CHRISTMAS

TO

KIMBERLY

THIS CERTIFICATE GOOD FOR

ONE HOUR OF CONVERSATION WITH YOUR FATHER TO TALK ABOUT LIFE!!!!!!!!

EXPIRES DECEMBER 31, 1999

IN PERSPECTIVE
◀◀ KOURTNEY ▶▶

A lot changed when my dad died. It made me think—you live your life and you buy this and this and that. But then when you die, what happens to all of it? You don't take it with you. It made me realize that life is more than material things. Instead of spending money on a handbag, I'd rather travel and spend money on other things that really add to who you are.

Since my dad's gone, I feel his energy, almost like he's making the decisions. And I definitely feel Dad's presence with Mason in my life.

When Dad was sick, Kim and Kourtney sat with him by the pool one night. They decided that if one of us passed away, the sign we'd give each other that we were okay in heaven would be a bird. After our dad passed, Kim was driving on the freeway and saw a huge flock of birds that made her stop the car. We knew that was our dad, saying, "I'm in heaven waiting for you."

The beliefs and integrity and confidence and love he gave us are far more valuable than houses or wealth or material possessions. He's still a huge presence in our lives, and we feel him looking over us and guiding us.

We miss you and love you, Daddy.

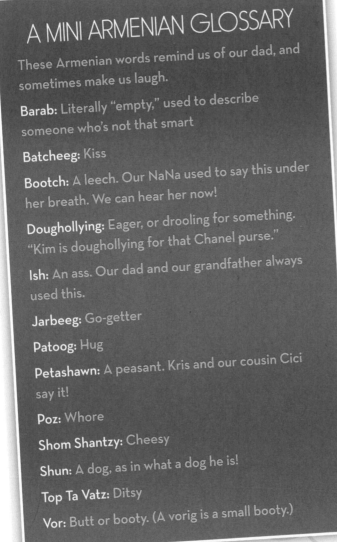

A MINI ARMENIAN GLOSSARY

These Armenian words remind us of our dad, and sometimes make us laugh.

Barab: Literally "empty," used to describe someone who's not that smart

Batcheeg: Kiss

Bootch: A leech. Our NaNa used to say this under her breath. We can hear her now!

Doughollying: Eager, or drooling for something. "Kim is doughollying for that Chanel purse."

Ish: An ass. Our dad and our grandfather always used this.

Jarbeeg: Go-getter

Patoog: Hug

Petashawn: A peasant. Kris and our cousin Cici say it!

Poz: Whore

Shom Shantzy: Cheesy

Shun: A dog, as in what a dog he is!

Top Ta Vatz: Ditsy

Vor: Butt or booty. (A vorig is a small booty.)

DADDY

Let It All OUT

Khloé: When Kourtney and Kim and I were called to Dad's house to say good-bye, the priest was there. Dad looked so little. He had a toy monkey when he was a kid that he named Jocko and he still had it in his bedroom closet. He asked for his Jocko, like he was a little boy. I went to get it and brought it to him.

Of all of us, I had the hardest time after our dad died. I wasn't able to talk about it at all, and I disappeared from my family. Whenever they mentioned him, I would cry hysterically and just have to leave. I didn't understand why God would let it happen. I got crazy with alcohol and became very self-destructive, and aggressive, too. I was always in a club, and the night would end with me angry and crying and screaming. I was mean and unhappy.

For the longest time I had absolutely terrifying dreams called night terrors to the point where I couldn't sleep. I got an ulcer. Oh, and I also lost all my hair. I had to wear a wig. It took two years for my hair to grow back, though some of it never did.

I blocked out so many things that happened. I hold too much in. I guess that's an understatement! On *Keeping Up*, they tried and tried to get me to talk about my dad on camera and I kept refusing, but finally I did it. It was the first time I had ever talked about him like that since he died, so in a way, it helped me. And I hoped it helped a lot of other people, too, with their own losses and pain.

I've tried to learn to express my emotions through writing. I liked to write poetry and stories as a kid, and I even had one published in the Marymount school newspaper. It really helps me to get my feelings down on paper.

After my dad died, I had to get a bunch of my things out of the house. I asked the woman he'd married if I could have Jocko, and for some reason she said no. When I was there packing up my own things, she was in the kitchen. So I just ran down the hall to his closet and grabbed Jocko out of the closet. I literally stole it! And while I was at it I also grabbed these boots my dad used to wear all the time. It was so worth it. I'm so glad to have a few things that he treasured, and especially old beat-up little Jocko.

We were celebrating Khloé's second birthday here so I would be about seven. — *Kourtney*

TOP TEN THINGS
OUR DAD TAUGHT US

Every year we skied in Vail, Colorado. Those trips are some of my fondest memories of my dad. In this picture I'm about seventeen. — *Kim*

Kourtney:

1. God has a plan for you.

2. Family is the most important thing in the world.

3. Money does NOT equal happiness.

4. Have a sense of humor. His was contagious!

5. Don't take yourself too seriously.

6. Have fun. He always told me not to get straight As if it meant not having fun . . . get Bs and have fun!

7. Treat people as you would like to be treated. He truly lived by this and treated EVERYONE with respect.

8. Give back and help others.

9. Make a soundtrack for your life. Music was playing at ALL times everywhere he could control it.

10. Be honest and loyal. He was a very honest and loyal man and those are qualities I take very seriously.

Dear Dad, (July 15, 1991)
What's up? How's life in Beverly Hills been lately? I recieved all Nine of yours and Denice's letters, And I thank you, I thank you, I thank you! Tell Kim that I got 2 of her letters and will write to her after this letter. Tell Robert that I recieved 1 of his letters, and could you please ask Khloe if she got the poster with dogs on it? At camp we trade stationary and I traded this for something of mine. I already can ski on "1" ski! I'm so happy! The food here is gross. But everything else is great! I know how to windsurf and sail. In ceramics I worked the wheel. (the wheel is what they did in "Ghost.") It's tons of fun! Call me when you get a chance, O.K. I've been saving all of the letters that I got!
Lot'za love,
Kourtney
PS: I got the candy you sent!
(THANKS)

Kim:

1. Never forget your heritage.

2. Blood is thicker than water, family comes first.

3. Be a hard worker, have a strong work ethic, and always give 100 percent.

4. Never get into drugs, alcohol, and smoking . . . he hated all of that like I do.

5. How to be silly and play practical jokes on everyone.

6. Save money.

7. Nothing comes easy.

8. Good morals

9. About Jesus and the Bible.

10. Be a good person and do unto others as you would have others do unto you.

Khloé:

1. Faith in your beliefs.

2. Loyalty.

3. Strong work ethic.

4. Family first.

5. Remember our heritage. It's part of what makes us who we are.

6. Don't be judgmental.

7. Money doesn't equal happiness.

8. Make serious moves but never be too serious yourself!

9. Everything happens for a reason.

10. Dance, smile, tell jokes, and laugh at yourself.

I always had frizzy, curly, big hair—I really didn't need the bow to top it off! That's *classic* Mom. I was about four here. My sisters played soccer and my dad coached them. During their games, I would play in the park, hit the ice cream truck, and get my face painted. — *Khloé*

When I was on *Dancing with the Stars* in 2008, my mom had these T-shirts made up. That's Rob's old girlfriend Adrienne at the far left, next to Kendall, and Kylie's next to my mom. — *Kim*

HOW TO GENERATE GIRL POWER

by Kim

I got divorced the year after my dad died. When you lose someone you love, it can help you see things clearly in your life. It helped me grow up and realize it was time to move on.

I've always been afraid to hurt people's feelings. And reluctant to say no when people ask me favors that I don't want to do. When I was younger I made decisions that I shouldn't have. I stayed with guys too long when they weren't treating me right. I wish I had listened to my parents. When **no one** in your family likes a person, there's got to be something to it.

But everything happens the way it should, because those experiences taught me a lot. I realized what I didn't want from life.

I was insecure sometimes when I was younger. I didn't really have any reason to be. I had a great family life with supportive parents who gave me attention, though there were so many kids around that sometimes I felt overwhelmed.

Sometimes I didn't feel skinny enough. I was always super-curvy, and you didn't see a lot of models or even celebrities with my kind of figure. Then this really great relationship I had in high school ended. I thought everything had been perfect and I didn't understand why we were breaking up, and it was really hard on me. From that moment on I began to feel a loss of self-esteem. And I gained a little bit of weight, maybe from trying to use food to comfort myself, and the extra weight made me feel worse.

After that I would date anyone who would give me attention. People that I knew on some level just weren't good for me. I knew I was unhappy, but I couldn't bring myself to say so. I might try to end the relationship but then I would hold back because I had such a difficult time coming out and saying something that might hurt someone else. I wasn't even thinking of my health or my mental health or anything.

It wasn't just guys. I let people treat me any way they wanted and never stood up for myself. I was a doormat.

I was very dependent on people, so I would go from boyfriend to boyfriend and never had a chance to be single.

After a few not-so-great relationships I decided I wanted to take a year off to be single. And you know what, I loved it! I loved hanging out with my girlfriends. I dove into traveling and I went all over the place—to Paris, Germany, Italy, and Australia. I went to all these different countries I never thought I would go to. My family had never been big on traveling abroad. When I traveled, it opened up my mind to a whole new world!

And then I started to get attention for my curves. Exactly the thing I'd been trying to get rid of for so long!

I used to think maybe I didn't attract the right kind of people because I didn't look the way they wanted me to. I hadn't figured out yet that the real reason I wasn't attracting the right kind of person was because I was such a people-pleaser. I wasn't strong enough to be the person I really am, and to insist on being with people who appreciated me that way. I truly think you get what you put out, and

> I WAS VERY DEPENDENT ON PEOPLE, SO I WOULD GO FROM BOYFRIEND TO BOYFRIEND AND NEVER HAD A CHANCE TO BE SINGLE.

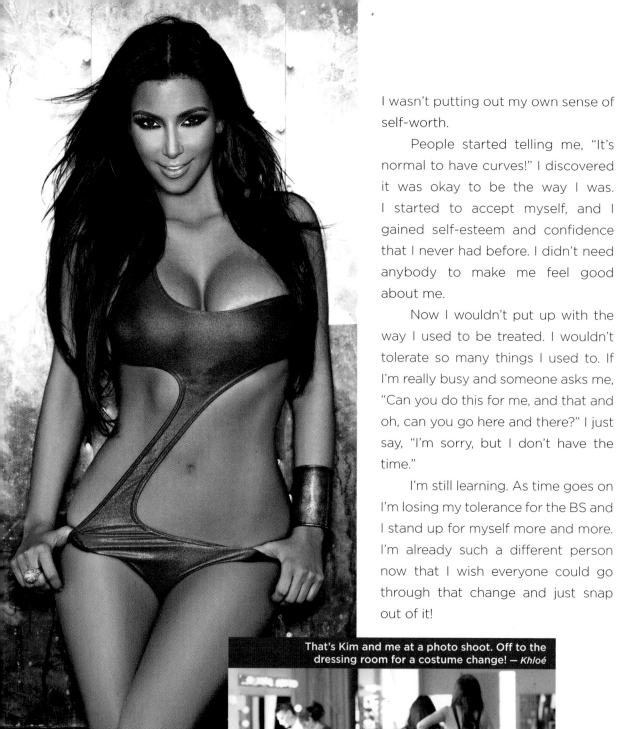

I wasn't putting out my own sense of self-worth.

People started telling me, "It's normal to have curves!" I discovered it was okay to be the way I was. I started to accept myself, and I gained self-esteem and confidence that I never had before. I didn't need anybody to make me feel good about me.

Now I wouldn't put up with the way I used to be treated. I wouldn't tolerate so many things I used to. If I'm really busy and someone asks me, "Can you do this for me, and that and oh, can you go here and there?" I just say, "I'm sorry, but I don't have the time."

I'm still learning. As time goes on I'm losing my tolerance for the BS and I stand up for myself more and more. I'm already such a different person now that I wish everyone could go through that change and just snap out of it!

That's Kim and me at a photo shoot. Off to the dressing room for a costume change! — *Khloé*

It's so important to have a strong sense of self-worth and confidence, and insist on being treated with respect. That means treating yourself with respect, too. I know how easy it is to be down on yourself, but you have to believe that you're a beautiful, worthwhile person who deserves the best. Remember, sometimes the thing you hate most about yourself is actually the thing that other people love most. Be proud of who you are, and definitely don't be with someone who doesn't totally adore you the way you are!

If I can tell you anything, something that I believe from the bottom of my heart, it's this: Always have the courage to be yourself. Completely.

JUST SAY NO!
◄◄ KOURTNEY ►►

You should know that Kim still has a problem turning people down when it comes to taking pictures or signing autographs. She doesn't want to disappoint any of her fans so even if she really needs to go she just cannot bring herself to cut it off. Everyone will be stopping to take pictures and tell stories and making her sign a million things, not just a piece of paper or a photo but their phones. Someone even brought a laptop once. I finally have to say, "Okay, that's enough! She has to be somewhere." Then I literally have to pull her away. Because she just can't say no!

9

SUDDEN-ONSET STARDOM

ometimes it's hard to believe how quickly all this happened. You know, how we became . . . *The* Kardashian Sisters. Yeah, we know we're celebrities, and there's no reason to be ashamed of it, but when you talk about yourself as a "celebrity" it's almost like you think you're better than everyone else. And we're not.

Kim was the one who first began getting a lot of attention out in public.

KIM: It started when I went out with Nick Lachey on a date. We went out to the movies in the afternoon, I think *The Da Vinci Code*. It was one of the first dates he'd been on since splitting up with Jessica Simpson, or at least the first time he'd been on a date publicly. Of course the paparazzi took pictures, because people were curious about who he was with. (We only went out for about a week.)

So the next night I was out with Paris Hilton and we were going to a club on Sunset. We were in her car and the paparazzi started taking pictures. Usually they would shout, "Paris! Paris! Paris!" But the night before they'd gotten these pictures of a mystery girl with Nick and by then they'd figured out who I was. So they started yelling, "Kim! Kim!" I wanted to hide, and Paris and I looked at each other and just laughed.

She said, "Whatever you do, just smile. And don't say anything under your breath because now they have video cameras, too." I thought, this is so weird, I don't know what's going on. It was surreal.

KHLOÉ: But when Kourtney and I got our first taste of fame it was not fun at all. It was like a bad taste you don't even want in your mouth! The three of us had driven down to San Diego to see our grandmother for a birthday lunch.

KOURTNEY: Then that night we went to a party Kim was hosting at some club, and photographers were there.

KHLOÉ: So the next morning a celebrity Web site had pictures of the two of us and said mean things like Kourtney was "rabbit-toothed" and I was "a fat transvestite."

KOURTNEY: Across my face it said "fugly." I remember thinking "nice, real nice." And it also said the two of us were like Arnold Schwarzenegger and Danny DeVito in the movie *Twins*.

KHLOÉ: Oh right! I really cried over that. And even a year later, remember Kourtney, after you were photographed at some event in New York? You were asking, "Do I look rabbit-toothed in this picture?"

KOURTNEY: The one thing that was really annoying at first was when people would say, "Oh, you're just trying to be your sister Kim."

KHLOÉ: And that was so not true. We are sisters, so we're kind of alike anyway, but we were just being ourselves! If anything, we were trying to show that we were doing things independently.

IN THE
PUBLIC EYE

It didn't take us long to learn that when you're in the public eye, a lot of people are going to say mean things about you, or things that just aren't true. At first it was hard, but we got used to it and after a while, we really didn't care. We don't expect everyone to like us. You can't please everyone.

Keeping Up with the Kardashians was popular right away but some people were very judgmental and thought we were just party girls who stayed out all night and slept all day. Then a lot of people saw the love that we have for each other and realized we go through so many of the same things they do.

Speaking of *Keeping Up*, you have to hear how the show happened in the first place. It came together so quickly it seriously boggled the mind. It wasn't too long after the media started following Kim.

One of our mom's best friends is Kathie Lee Gifford. She's on the *Today* show and she's also the godmother of our little sisters Kendall and Kylie. She's great, really fun, and a truly good person who's raised amazing kids. She's very religious, and unlike most of our mom's friends, she likes to talk about religion. We usually only see her a couple times a year, but we see her now more often because we go on her show.

This was at my mom's birthday dinner at the restaurant XIV. We ran into family friend Lionel Richie there and took a pic! — *Kourtney*

Whenever Kathie Lee would visit us, she'd say, "You are such a crazy family! Where are the cameras? We need cameras in here!" She thought our family would make a really funny show. So my mom went to Ryan Seacrest with the idea and he loved it. And literally a week later we had all these people with cameras in our house filming, and it was on the air really soon after that.

Kim: It happened so fast, we really didn't know what we were doing. Then right after we began filming I was asked to pose in *Playboy*. I was hesitant at first—my sisters will tell you I'm very shy and I don't feel that comfortable even talking about sex—but my mom was like, "You should! It will be amazing!" *Playboy* is iconic.

I know my dad would have hated me posing for *Playboy*. One time someone we knew posed for *Playboy* and he was disgusted. I remember he said, "Now her daughter has to go to school knowing those pictures of her mother are out there!"

I knew Dad wouldn't approve, but I thought, "I'm an adult now and I'm allowed to make the choice." So I finally said yes. It was such a great experience, and working with Hugh Hefner was unforgettable.

I'm glad we showed me overcoming my fears on the show. Still, I was really glad the show was going to be about my whole family and not just about me, because in no way could I carry it by myself. I'm boring, but I knew that people would fall in love with my sisters and their wild and crazy sides.

I went to a Save the Seals event given by PETA and Nigel Barker, a photographer who did a documentary on seals and how they're killed for their coats. I was all glammed up to bring awareness to a good cause. — *Khloé*

Khloé: Each of us has a particular personality from the show that people identify us with. For example, I'm the outrageous, feisty one. It's true that I'm more vocal and vulgar than my sisters, but sometimes when people meet me in person, they're so shocked, they say, "You're so different than we thought. You're actually calm! Instead of being the instigator you seem to be the mediator." Well, what do they want me to do, swear at them? Of course I say crazy things around my family because with them I'm in a comfort zone.

Kourtney:

I think people probably didn't know what to make of me the first season, because I was definitely the most closed-off of the three of us. Like when Scott and I decided all of a sudden to get married in Las Vegas, you couldn't tell from the show how upset I was about the whole thing. I ran off-camera to the bathroom and was just sitting there crying my eyes out.

I wasn't like Khloé, who is always just herself and didn't care about the cameras. I didn't know how much of what was filmed would end up on the show. At the end of the day I'd come home and go over every little thing, like, "I can't believe I said that!" I was worried that people would think I was dumb or get the wrong impression.

But then once I started seeing the show, I was fine. And after a while, you become incapable of censoring yourself for twelve to eighteen hours a day!

The show did take a bit of getting used to, not just for Kourtney but for all of us. And fame, if you want to call it that, was definitely an adjustment at first. There was an episode where we were giving Kim a hard time for letting fame go to her head and being a diva. But really it was that the whole family was going through a period of adjustment, because it was new to all of us. We're still learning as we go. Trust us, our family is so close that no one would ever have the chance to get too diva-ish!

Sometimes the tabloids will say things like "The Kardashian Sisters Are at Each Other's Throats!" and run stories about how we're all jealous of each other and fighting. Which is so ridiculous it's a joke. We laugh at that stuff. If there was one thing our parents taught us, it was to stick together as family, and be supportive of one another. We're thrilled when one of us does well. If anything, it motivates us to work harder. After the first season or two of *Keeping Up With the Kardashians*, when E! said they wanted to do *Kourtney and Khloé Take Miam*i, all three of us were excited.

Our attitude is, There's plenty to go around. We say, "Yay!" when something good happens to one of us, because it's kind of like something good happens to all of us.

Khloé and I played flag football at an event during the Superbowl in Tampa. We had the time of our lives! — *Kourtney*

BFFS, FRENEMIES, AND FORMER FRIENDS

Kim: You probably know what it's like when you're really good friends with a person, but then things change, and you just can't be as close to them anymore. Like when they do something to betray your friendship. It just happens sometimes.

I guess a frenemy is when you can still be kinda friends with that person, but you have to watch out for them and be careful not to reveal too much or let yourself be vulnerable. Because you're never really sure if they're your friend or not.

I can't have frenemies. I tend to be emotional, and I feel strongly about the people I'm close to. It's very hard for me to let go of relationships, but if someone has been really mean to me and crushed our bond, I eventually have to let go of them completely.

I think when your life changes, you yourself don't necessarily change, but the people around you sometimes do. Some people have a hard time dealing with someone else's good fortune. After we started doing *Keeping Up*, a few people would say negative things about us, maybe not to our faces, but behind our backs. Or even try to sabotage us. As sad as it is, sometimes you just have to let people go. It's really difficult to say good-bye to someone that you've loved, but then it's such a relief not to have that negativity in your life anymore.

I don't believe you should speak badly of other people. I don't go around talking trash about former friends. I just try not to talk about them at all. It's better to take the high road.

BACK TO SCHOOL

Khloé: You know how it is when you're criticized, that's all you remember, even if good things are said about you, too? At first, when pictures of me would come out and people would say mean things, I almost felt like my school life was starting all over again. You know, having to hear all the time "I can't believe you're related to Kim and Kourtney!" And at first I was known as the "fat, funny one" on the show. But my school experience from way back when taught me how to handle it, and after about a month I got my confidence back. And, I wasn't even fat, I was normal.

Still, my own experience really made me realize that you have to be careful about what you say when everyone will hear it, or read it. Like bullies who post nasty things about classmates online—that can be really hurtful and lead to true tragedy. It's never nice to talk trash about someone. I know it's hard not to sometimes, especially when they deserve it! But I try to remember how I used to be so hurt by the negative things people said about me. So especially if I'm online, where I know millions of people now and into the future could potentially see what I say, I try to be careful. You know—if you can't say something nice, don't say anything at all. Word.

> STILL, MY OWN EXPERIENCE REALLY MADE ME REALIZE THAT YOU HAVE TO BE CAREFUL ABOUT WHAT YOU SAY WHEN EVERYONE WILL HEAR IT OR READ IT.

TALK IT THROUGH

Kourtney: The show is kind of like therapy. We do normally hang out together just as much as we do on the show, but when there's a camera crew there, it forces you to deal with any issues you have. Especially when we sit down to do the interviews where we talk about what happened and how we're feeling. Instead of just pushing it aside or forgetting about it, we have to really face things and try to figure them out.

It's also nice that with the show our lives are documented, because we can watch the episodes later and see how we've grown and changed. And I think we're all better at confronting our issues now, too, even without the show, because we've learned how much it helps to acknowledge your feelings and deal with them. It turns out you don't need a camera to do that!

Oh my goodness, this event was ages ago! It was for T-Mobile Side-kick and I'm wearing Diane von Furstenberg. Rob was with us—it was the night he met his ex-girlfriend Adrienne for the first time. — *Khloé*

LET'S Get Real

Yes, we've heard it. You know, when people say, "Why are those girls famous?" Or a variation: "They're just famous for being famous." (Um, what does that mean, anyway?)

We're not big fans of the word *famous*. Or really, we should say we're not big fans of using it when we're talking about ourselves. It makes us sound conceited. We were raised not to judge people based on status or wealth or possessions. And we certainly weren't taught to think we were better than anyone else. You'll never hear us saying, "Oh, we're celebrities now, so you have to bow to us and do everything for us." Truly, we are not that into ourselves. We are definitely recognizable, though. That's a good way to put it.

We used to have movie night with our dad once a week and we'd watch old movies. So we grew up loving movie stars like Audrey Hepburn and Marilyn Monroe. We're definitely a different kind of celebrity from them. We're not actresses or performers. We are business women, sisters, a mother, a wife, entrepreneurs, fashion designers! (Though Kim has dabbled in acting.) And we didn't set out to be celebrities. We're just living our lives, and our claim to recognizability is that we do it in front of the cameras, and people like watching it.

Look, people will say mean things about you no matter what job you're in. You can have your own TV show or be working at Starbucks. You just can't please everybody, and you can't let it rule your life.

Reality TV is strange, because the people who watch it feel like they truly know you, more than they would actors in a sitcom or something. Especially with reality shows like ours, where it's like you're right there with us day to day as we go about our usual business. Like one night Malika and Lamar and I were leaving a Lakers game, driving Kim to her car in a parking structure across the street. She started screaming "Go, Lakers!" (You wouldn't believe it was soft-spoken little Kim screaming, she's so loud. She used to do it to

Rob at his games just to be evil.) Fans noticed it was us in the car so they started chasing us. We thought it was so fun! We were laughing so hard we almost cried. But once we drove up three levels in the parking garage and a group of people were still chasing us, it got a little scary. We were glad Lamar was there—he was ready to protect his family!

We feel so lucky to have a reality show like ours, because if you were doing it with strangers or even friends, it would be such a different dynamic. We're with family, so it's very comfortable, first of all. And every one of us is 100 percent sure of each other's support. We genuinely love one another and want the very best for one another. If we didn't have that kind of relationship, things could get very competitive and nasty.

Run's House is fun to watch because it's a family, too, and it's interesting to see how everyone relates to each other. If we had to say who we were most like, it would be *The Osbournes*, because they were wacky, too; but they all loved each other a lot. And we're a little bit like *The Brady Bunch*, because you know, it was the story of a lucky lady who was bringing up three girls on her own. And then she married a guy who had three boys. And we also identify with *The Sound of Music,* because there are just so many of us! So *The Osbournes* crossed with *The Sound of Music.* Someone told us once we reminded them of *I Love Lucy,* which is one of Khloé's all-time favorites. So Khloé would be Lucy, because she's always cooking up schemes, Kourtney would be Ethel, because she goes along with Khloé's craziness, and Kim would be Ricky because she's always rolling her eyes and scolding Lucy and Ethel. And Fred? Hmmm. Rob can be kind of cranky sometimes. Rob would have to be Fred!

Kim and I went to Australia in 2007 to present at their MTV video awards and while we were there we went to the zoo in Sydney. The kangaroo was the cutest ever—I danced with him! We weren't allowed to hold the koala because they can get a little feisty. Kim got a little too close and he tried to claw her. — *Khloé*

COWGIRL
by Kourtney

Keeping Up with the Kardashians actually wasn't the first reality show I ever did. A few years before that, I was on another E! series called *Filthy Rich: Cattle Drive*.

It wasn't that long after my dad had died, and I was living with my boyfriend at the time. My life was very orderly and very routine. I was doing Smooch and coming home and that's about it. My best friend wanted to be on the show and asked me to do it with her. I said, "Absolutely not!" She thought it would be good for me, but I didn't want to do it. I thought it was so lame that everyone wanted to be on a TV show. I didn't want to be famous.

Courtenay—yes, we basically had the same name—really pressured me to go with her, though, so I went. I told the producers I thought the whole thing was embarrassing and I did not want to do it. So when I got a call from them saying, "Pack your bags!" I said no.

But then one day I woke up and thought, I'm going to do it. I wanted to do it for the experience. So I went to Colorado, where there was this ranch up in the mountains. If I hadn't, when else would I have even dared to sleep in a tent for three weeks? The boys were in one tent and the girls were in another. And we had to do all sorts of things. We ate every night by the campfire. There was no access to mirrors—for three weeks all we had was our little makeup mirrors—and no sinks or running water for brushing your teeth, so we used bottled water. And we had to use a Porta-Potty. It was truly reality out on the range.

The first day my jeans were so tight I couldn't spread my legs far enough to get on the horse! I had no idea how to get on a horse in the first place, but I learned, and we had to learn to saddle our horses and groom them. We

OUR FAVORITE ACTRESSES FROM THE SILVER SCREEN

◄◄ KOURTNEY ►►

Audrey Hepburn

Bette Davis

◄◄ KIM ►►

Elizabeth Taylor

Sophia Loren

◄◄ KHLOÉ ►►

Marilyn Monroe

Doris Day

Audrey Hepburn

Ann-Margret

> THE FIRST DAY MY JEANS WERE SO TIGHT I COULDN'T SPREAD MY LEGS FAR ENOUGH TO GET ON THE HORSE!

delivered a baby calf. We killed and skinned and ate a rattlesnake—it tasted like chicken. I even ate cow's balls! Which also kind of tasted like chicken.

We'd spend all day herding, and the whole thing ended up on the Fourth of July with us parading the cows down the streets of Steamboat Springs. I said almost nothing during filming, so I was barely on the show, but I was just thrilled with the whole experience.

OMG THAT WAS SO EMBARRASSING!

Kourtney, Scott, and I went to the Bahamas and visited an aquarium. This is by the shark tank. — *Kim*

Everyone does things to embarrass themselves. We, of course, are no exception. The only difference is when we mess up it's in front of, like, everyone on the planet. At least it feels that way.

Now if you've made a relatively minor boo-boo, like wearing an outfit that you had no idea would be so see-through—and believe us, honey, we've been there—then you should just get over it. Yeah, you might get a few snickers. Or you might not even know your bra and panties were clearly visible under your dress until you go online one day. Not fun. But you'll live. No one really got hurt in the making of that photograph, except your ego.

The worst, though, is when you screw up big-time and majorly embarrass yourself to the point where you want to move to a tiny country no one's ever heard of. In that situation, we've discovered it's best to follow six simple rules:

1. Hold your head high.

2. Take responsibility.

3. Get through it by making the best of it.

4. Rely on your support system (in our case, our family).

5. Learn from it.

6. Move on.

We've also discovered that when you make those kinds of mistakes, it can be painful to the people you love. That of course makes you feel even worse, but then you feel better when you realize they've got your back.

If you've seen our shows you know we've made embarrassing mistakes. (We'd really rather not go over them yet another time here, because the show is a constant reminder. Like, okay, you really don't want to do that again!) In every one of those situations, we turned to our family to help us through. Even if it seemed at first like Mom and Bruce and various siblings were piling on, we trusted them and we knew they loved us, and in the end, we leaned on them for support.

The most important thing is learning from your mistakes. Even with that surprisingly sheer outfit, you hopefully know that next time you better have someone check you out before you head out the door.

If your behavior really casts doubt on your judgment and maturity, well, then there's just a bigger lesson to learn. Simple.

Ultimately, embarrassment is just a fleeting thing. Who cares about what other people think? The opinions you should value are yours, and those of people you love and trust.

Take your punishment, learn your lesson, and get on with your life.

CALL A CAB

Khloé: I don't mind talking about the dumb things I've done because, well, you know I'm pretty open and out there with everything. I don't believe in tiptoeing around sensitive topics, especially if they're important.

In the first season of *Keeping Up* we did a show about my DUI, aka Driving Under the Influence (of booze). One night I was out partying and had too many drinks to get behind the wheel of my car. Mind you, I didn't realize it when I got into my car, but that's the thing about drinking—it plays with your head, so sometimes you think you're okay to drive when you're not.

If you saw that episode, you know I had to stay overnight in jail, which was hideous. And I was required to take classes and do community service. Even Donald Trump put his two cents in on my crime and punishment: He fired me from *Celebrity Apprentice* when he found out that I'd gotten a DUI, even though it happened months and months before that. And in spite of the fact that I wasn't underage when it happened, and that I was taking responsibility and trying to make up for it. I thought that was a bit much, but hey, he's the Donald and it was his show.

In any case, that DUI truly taught me a life-and-death lesson. I never, ever drink and drive anymore. In a way, I thank God for the experience because I probably would have gone on doing it without being aware of how much I was endangering myself and others.

Preach.

IN ANY CASE, THAT DUI TRULY TAUGHT ME A LIFE-AND-DEATH LESSON. I NEVER, EVER DRINK AND DRIVE ANYMORE. IN A *WAY*, I THANK GOD FOR THE EXPERIENCE BECAUSE I PROBABLY WOULD HAVE GONE ON DOING IT WITHOUT BEING AWARE OF HOW MUCH I *WAS* ENDANGERING MYSELF AND OTHERS.

We went on vacation in Puerto Vallarta, Mexico, in 2007 and went zip-lining through a rain forest. It was amazing! This was in the truck on the way up the mountain. — *Khloé*

MOM, MOMAGER, THE FABULOUS KRIS JENNER

When we were kids, we called our mom "Mom" to her face. But behind her back . . . We're kidding, we don't talk about her behind her back. We tell her to her face whatever we're thinking, in case you hadn't noticed! We're just saying it was the same with our mom as with our dad: We referred to him as Daddy and we referred to Mom as Mommy. Now as you know we still call her Mom, or Kris. And Khloé sometimes calls her "The Fabulous Kris Jenner," because Khloé says she's too glam and fabulous to just be Mom— and because it's just fun to say. And because she manages our careers, she's our momager, too!

Kris was younger than most of our friends' mothers when we were kids, at least when Kourtney and Kim were. She was a really cool mom. She blasted great music in the car and cooked all the time and took Kourtney's Brownie troops on camping trips, but not to the wilderness—to fabulous hotels. Instead of hiking, we'd go to SeaWorld.

She had the most fabulous clothes. When we were little, we used to play in her closet. Or her bathroom, because she had the best makeup, like this YSL lipstick with a jewel on top.

My mom and I were posing before I went to my boyfriend's prom. It was the first time I wore an expensive dress by Mark Wong Nark. I was so scared to ask my mom to buy it for me. It was the first time I had my hair and makeup done, too! — *Kim*

Mom showed us how we want to be with our own daughters. Even with things that seem small but are important. For example, she taught us about grooming. She was really into being clean and taking care of her skin. She'd tell us to use hot, hot water with a washcloth to get all our makeup off, and she always used glycerin soap. She said all the stewardesses used to buy Erno Laszlo skin products. She taught us to always put on lotion when you get out of the shower, and clean your ears every day. And when you brush your teeth, brush your tongue and the roof of your mouth, too, because that's where the bacteria are. She took us to have manis and pedis every week.

We really appreciate all that from her, because it taught us how to respect our bodies, and to always want to look our best.

And she worked hard to make a great home for her family. She was organized like our dad, and she was very big on presentation, so we always grew up in a beautiful environment. She always wanted the very best for us. Even back then she loved clothes and getting all dolled up. We're quite sure we inherited our shopping gene from her! She says before she married our dad, he was kind of cheap. But not after.

Both of our parents were so strong on family values and confidence, and emphasizing responsibility and the importance of hard work. One of her rules was, "If you want 'extras' you're on your own." Meaning, she'd buy us our underwear and our basics, but if we were heading to the designer section of the store, we were on our own. She was the one who indoctrinated us into the cult of clothing, but then if we wanted to-die-for clothes, *we* had to come up with the cash! It was so maddening at the time, but that rule is probably why we have so many to-die-for clothes today!

Mom always made us feel totally comfortable around her. We could say anything we wanted and never had to stifle ourselves.

So with that in mind . . .

Let's face it, Kris *can* be kind of exhausting. She's very passionate about everything, whether it be bad or good. It's fun to see, but sometimes you think, take a chill pill.

Sometimes people who watch our shows think I'm not close to my mother, but that couldn't be further from the truth! I may not be quite the mommy's girl I used to be when I was a kid, but Kris and I are tight. — *Khloé*

For instance, sometimes she starts telling us things in what we call her "infomercial voice." She uses this TV kind of tone and talks to us like she's selling us a product.

Say it's a bowl. She'll be like, "Oh my God, I saw the most gorgeous bowl at the Ivy! It reminded me of when your dad and I were on our honeymoon in 1972! And it's to die, it has this and that and blah blah blah and on and on." After a while we're, "Okay, Kris, yeah, yeah. Just buy the freakin' bowl already!"

She has these Hermès dishes that she loves. They're special-occasion dishes, really expensive. You don't just go out and buy the whole set—you get one of them a year, or every now and then. So when people come to the house, she accosts them and starts running around, showing them her dishes and explaining them in detail. Which is kind of adorable. All of our friends love her. Everyone says, "Oh, your mom is so cute!" But if it's your mom, of course you tease her.

One of the best things about Kris is that she's very fun. If she's having a barbecue and a bunch of our friends are there, and maybe we're doing shots, we'll try to get her to join in. We'll say, "Take a shot, Mom!" She'll be, "I don't want to!" But then she gives in. (It's funny, we can get our mom to do shots but not Kim, because she hardly ever drinks.) We wouldn't want a mom who always acted old.

People sometimes say, "Oh you're so mean to your mom, you need to be more respectful." And sometimes

ALL OF OUR FRIENDS LOVE HER. EVERYONE SAYS, "OH, YOUR MOM IS SO CUTE!" BUT IF IT'S YOUR MOM, OF COURSE YOU TEASE HER.

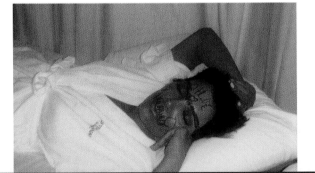

We were on a girls' vacation at Las Ventanas in Cabo San Lucas, Mexico, and all of us—except Kim, of course—had a little too much fun this night. I think it was in 2005. My mom went to sleep in spite of Kourt and me playing around and making noise, so we decided to write on her face with an eyeliner pen. She literally had no idea at all we were doing it and couldn't figure out why we were laughing when she woke up! — *Khloé*

when we watch the show, we think, "Ooh, we were kind of mean." But that's just the way we are in our family. We say what we're feeling. She thinks we're very hard on her, but she forgets we're her daughters, and that's how daughters are with their moms. That's how she is with her own mom!

This was filmed for *Keeping Up*. My mom was going through some kind of a midlife crisis and would not leave us alone for anything in the world, so we rented a monkey for a week to occupy her time. — *Khloé*

And then there's the fact that we have a business relationship with her. Having a momager definitely muddies things a little. When we seem harsh with Kris it's usually over something having to do with that. The times we don't communicate very well are when we're speaking to our manager, and she's reacting as our mom.

Like if we're unhappy about a business deal she's made and she says, "I have six kids and I'm doing this and that trying to get everything done . . ." And gets all upset. That's blurring the line, and you have to say, "You're my manager now, so that's not relevant." Because if your manager isn't your mom and maybe works in some corporation, if you ask them to do something, they won't go into their family obligations and personal life.

We do tend to be very direct, especially if it's business-related. Like at Dash, we don't go around saying, "Hey, honey pie, could you pretty please hang this dress over there?" We say, "Put those hangers there, steam this." When Kourtney hires new girls to work at the store, she always gives them the talk: "This isn't the time to be sensitive, we're all just working here."

Of course you don't want your daughter yelling at you, but when you're also her manager, you have to separate the two. It's a very fine line, though. It has to be hard for her not to take things personally. And we must admit, we probably yell at her more easily because she's our mom. We trust her more than we would a regular manager, but we wouldn't get so intense with someone else.

Kris is a perfectionist, and sometimes she just takes on too much without getting other people to help her. (A perfectionist? Who else do we know like that? Oh right, her three oldest daughters!) Sometimes it's tricky having a momager, but we wouldn't want it any other way.

We love you just as you are, Mom!

IN SYNC

◀◀◀ KIM ▶▶▶

My mom and I are a lot alike in the way we approach business. So we communicate well, probably the best out of my sisters. Kourtney is probably the worst. Sometimes when Kourtney needs to ask my mom to do something, she'll have Khloé ask for her, because Khloé will put it more diplomatically. When I'm on a tight schedule sometimes I get angry and emotional with Mom. Khloé and Kourtney always want a clear separation between work and personal with Mom, but I don't worry about that so much. Mom and I are both workaholics. We could work on Christmas Day and it wouldn't bother us.

Kimberly,   2003

Happy
Valentine's Day,
Your
Wonderfulness!

I love you so much...
I am so proud of who
you are and am so blessed
to have you as a
daughter ♡
You are my heart ♡
mommy XOXOXO

Ya Gotta
HAVE FAITH

When we were kids, our mom did Bible study every week and we always went to Sunday school. Our family went to Bel Air Presbyterian, including our dad, because he liked to worship with us all. And then we'd go to brunch afterward, or to our grandparents' for lunch. As we got older, we got away from going to church every week, but lately we've been going more often.

For a while my mom was going to this church in the Valley that she loved, where she really felt a connection with the minister, Pastor Brad. One Sunday the pastor wasn't there, then the next Sunday, too. My mom kept going back hoping to find him, but apparently he'd quit the church after some personal problems. Though Kris really tried to maintain her bond with that church, she just couldn't, so she tried others. But it just wasn't the same.

Then one night she had a dream telling her to open up a church with Pastor Brad. When she woke up, she knew she had to do it. She immediately started the search for Pastor Brad. Eventually, she learned he was working at a Starbucks. She

didn't know his shift, though, so Bruce stopped at that Starbucks twice a day looking for him, every day for three months. Finally he found him! My mom convinced Pastor Brad to join her on her mission, so she helped him back to his faith and they started up their own church. They began having services at a movie theater at the Calabasas Commons shopping center, and soon lots of people began coming. It's a wonderful church, not all high and mighty, just come as you are. That's where we go to church now, and Pastor Brad even married Khloé and Lamar.

FAIR Fight

Khloé: Whenever we have arguments, we get everyone involved. Like if I get mad at Kim, Kim will call Kourtney and complain. And then Kourtney will call me, and blah! blah! blah!

Some people say that Kourtney and I pick on Kim. Kourtney and I do team up together but we don't gang up on Kim. It's just that she's more sensitive, and emotional and dramatic. And it's not two against one either because she has Kris. Kris will almost always stand up for her and take her side and yell at us.

My mom and Kim are like identical twins. They are the exact same. It's not that my mom loves any one of us more than the others. But she does give a little extra attention to Kim. That's okay because I think parents instinctively know what each kid needs. I was always a little more distant and independent. Kourtney, if you tried to give her as much attention as Kim gets, she wouldn't even let you. She'd think you were weird. So Kim gets more emphasis because that's what Kim wants and needs.

Kourtney: When we have fights in our family, they usually don't end with an apology. Instead, you just make up by getting back to normal. Like you'll call and say, "You want to go shopping?" Or you send a text saying, "Oh my God, guess what just happened!" We really don't say "I'm sorry" very much. That's just the way we are.

GROW UP
ALREADY

KIM: Sometimes my sisters embarrass me.

KOURTNEY: You mean when we make stuff up? Like that time we were at a party and we were bored so we just did the red carpet for an hour and told random stories?

KIM: Yes, that kind of thing can be embarrassing.

KHLOÉ: We were telling people we were kissing bandits who just went around making out with anyone we saw.

KOURTNEY: We were just literally making it all up. And they were writing it all down!

KIM: Like that totally gross thing you two were talking about on an *E! News* interview one time. It was disgusting.

KHLOÉ: Ask Kourtney about that. I don't know where that came from. But I am very good at making up stories.

123

KIM: You two think it's funny when you say outrageous, totally made-up things or act like little kids, but sometimes you just don't understand it's not the right time or place.

KHLOÉ: Kim is always apologizing for us.

KOURTNEY: Once Khloé and I pretended to be stylists. We met this photographer on a plane and we just went on and on about being stylists.

KHLOÉ: I was a teenager and a pathological liar, but Kourtney, you were an adult and you were lying, too. What's up with that?

KOURTNEY: So he called us to do a job. We were gonna say no but he offered us $1,500.

KHLOÉ: We went into a panic and just started pulling clothes and shoes from our own closets.

KOURTNEY: We had no idea what we were doing! And then we couldn't believe it—he said after that we were the most professional people they'd ever worked with. They called us to do another job but we said no. We didn't want to push our luck.

KIM: And what about the way you two are always wrestling and hitting each other and goofing around?

KOURTNEY: You know, that only started in maybe the last five years. I think when we started living together.

I have this picture in my office—it says everything about us! It's from Vegas probably in 2006. What a night! I'm just being free, enjoying my life to the fullest, and Kim is so disturbed at me she's almost in shock. And Rob is having a ball. This shot is priceless to me! — *Khloé*

KHLOÉ: Kourtney's always been so much smaller than me, and I find it so entertaining to just grab her and hold her like she's my doll. The other day we were on a boat and I was like, "Come here, my little baby," and I was cradling her.

KOURTNEY: You weren't allowed to do that when I was pregnant, because you can get a little rough.

KHLOÉ: Well, of course I never want to hurt you. I know my own strength. When we wrestle, you usually start it. You'll smack my ass really hard and then I'm like, "Ow!" And I hit you back. I always let you get rougher first because you're smaller. And then you have that move of yours, Kourtney. Do it!

KOURTNEY: No, you just tell what it is.

KHLOÉ: She psychs you out. She pretends she's hitting you in the face but she hits you in the stomach and it knocks the air out of you. But I still laugh. I find it so funny. Her really good secret weapon, though, are those claws of hers. She'll dig her nails into you until the bitter end, until she has no nails left.

KOURTNEY: But the other day we were in a photo shoot, while they were actually taking pictures, and you just hauled off and socked me in the arm.

KHLOÉ: You poked me in the eye!

KOURTNEY: I was just trying to brush something out of your eye.

KHLOÉ: Well, there's an eye in my eye!

KOURTNEY: Usually it ends with me over her knee and finally I tell her it hurts, I can't move.

KHLOÉ: And I say, "I'll let you go if you tell me you love me."

KOURTNEY: So I say, "I love you."

KHLOÉ: And then she has to give me a reason that she loves me. And then I let her go.

KIM: What are you two, like, ten years old? Honestly.

127

BIRTHDAY GiRLs

She rarely passed gas, but when she did, it came out pink and glittery, and it smelled like candy, and people cried when it went away.

Happy Birthday, Sis

Happy Birthday Kourt! I'm sorry I can't be here to celebrate with you, but I hope today is magical! I love you very much!
♥ Kim

We love treating each other on our birthdays. And our mom and Kendall and Kylie and our girlfriends! Our number-one priority on someone's big day is making her feel special—and making sure she has fun! Here's what we like to do:

Hey, Sis--
Remember all the goofy clothes

You can stop now.

Happy Birthday

Dear Khloé-
Happy 15th b-day!
Only 1 more year until you can drive!
I love you
♡
Kim

Khlo-Ball,

Happy Birthday,
Gorgeous

You are amazing! You are the best sister, sista'... my little twinkie, pop tart muffin, golden sparkling gem drop, good rad toasted bun seed, plum tart strudle ball... I can go on for decades, the adjectives keep coming!
I love you! Kourt

Khloé:

Give her a note that's handwritten with love and feeling.

Send balloons or flowers or cupcakes, something in her style that shows you thought of her specifically.

Take her to her favorite restaurant for lunch or dinner.

Kourtney:

Take her to a fun girls' lunch.

Get in some good old-fashioned shopping.

Spend some special girls' time together.

Kim:

Ask her straight up what she wants the most and get that gift for her.

Write a nice, long card—that's the most special gift!

HAPPY BIRTHDAY!

Khloe— 2002

Happy Birthday! I can't believe you are 18 years old! I always thought of you as my little sister but not anymore! Lately we have gotten so close, you really are my best friend and that makes me so happy! I have so much fun with you all the time. Never change, you are so beautiful and so much fun to be with! I love you so much and I am so excited to go out tonight for your birthday! I love you so much, thanks for always being there

—Kimberly

DELIGHT YOURSELF IN THE LORD AND HE WILL
GIVE YOU THE DESIRES OF YOUR HEART
—Psalm 37:4

Kourtney   11.2.06

Cool boots

Or at least kick it really hard. Cabo! Can't wait!!... i love you so so much and i just want to let you know you are such a huge huge part of me... i am so blessed to have you to share my life with, and i adore every minute we spend together. You are an amazing girl, and i treasure you♥

mommy xoxo

May ... be as full a ... ful as you are!

Just as there is no way to measure all the happiness you've given, there are no words to tell you how special you are and how very much you're loved.

Happy Birthday

there are no words to explain how much i love you. You have grown into such an amazing fabulous woman and i have learned so much from watching you mature. You have given me so much joy in my life and my blessing every day is the privaledge of seeing your smile every morning as we work together. I want you to know how grateful i am for all

---

the help you have given me lately spiritually, emotionally and of course my cars. I appreciate your kindness + love & just want you to know how much i love & adore you. You are my gift & i will always thank God he gave me you first.

♥ i love you madly ♥

mommy
xoxoxo

INSANITY
IS DOING THE SAME THING OVER and OVER AGAIN, but EXPECTING DIFFERENT [RE]SULTS.

Happy Birthday
Woman

♥

Kourt—
Sometimes i swear you are nuts! But you are still one of my favorites. I love how crazy and silly you are. Happy Birthday to my little chipmunck! This is going to be a memorable year for all of us, so get ready WOMAN!! I love you so much. Thanks for always being there for me.

xoxo
Khloé

This is us on the set of our photo shoot for our book cover!
— Kourtney, Kim, and Khloé

11

CELEBRITY RULES

We won't lie to you. Being a celebrity can be pretty fabulous.

It's fun to travel and do new things and meet all sorts of people. We get to wear to-die-for clothes and go to great parties and stay in fab hotels. And who doesn't like getting a little attention? We enjoy a lot of perks, and we know how lucky we are.

The most incredible thing, the thing that really amazes us, is all of our fans, and the positive energy they give us.

So first of all, to our fans out there, thank you *so* much. We really appreciate you guys more than anything.

But let's be honest: Being a celebrity is a job. And like any job, it has its downsides. We don't pretend that we're slaving away at hard labor, but sometimes our work can be exhausting and frustrating. And dangerous— because if you fall into the trap of taking yourself too seriously, you risk getting a very swollen head.

In our relatively short but illuminating time in the celebrity world, we've come up with some do's and don'ts and other guidelines. They're based on our personal experiences as both celebrities *and* fans. Because of course we're fans, too, of a lot of singers and actors and other cool people.

HOW TO BE A CELEB

1. Get over yourself.

A big reason that people like us is that they identify with us. We remind them of their own families! We enjoy being sisters the same way sisters everywhere do, and we have the same kinds of fights and deal with the same kinds of issues within our family. We don't like show-offs and we don't want to be the kind of celebrities who go around bragging about what we have or setting ourselves off from other people.

2. Treat people with respect.

We're all about respect, and we treat others the way we expect to be treated. It doesn't matter who a person is or what they do for a living. Our dad taught us that. We're not rude and condescending to other people. And we don't expect people to kiss our butts, either. In fact, we don't want people kissing up to us. That's fake. They're not really interacting with us, they're just someone treating us differently because we're celebs.

3. Do the right thing.

Our parents always taught us to have compassion for people less fortunate than we were. When we were kids our dad gave us this book called *The Richest Man in Babylon*. It teaches that you can only be the richest man if you're not greedy, and you give to others. Our dad always gave 10 percent of his earnings to the church.

When you're a celebrity, it's doubly important to give back, because you have an opportunity to set an example. We give a percentage of our earnings to the Dream Foundation, which grants wishes to terminally ill adults, and every month we do these big eBay charity auctions. Khloé helped build a home in New Orleans with Habitat for Humanity after Hurricane Katrina. She highlights a different charity every Monday on her blog.

Sometimes we'll do charity events and it just breaks your heart, but warms your heart at the same time. Like when we went to St. Jude's and met this little girl, Anna, who had cancer. When we give back, we get back something, too.

4. Keep it in perspective.

It's great that we're on TV and running around having our pictures taken and all that, but who's to say it will last forever? It might—Mom says that in 2020 she wants to be doing *Keeping Up with the Kardashians Season 24: Kylie Gets Married*. But seriously. We don't know what will happen in the future and we want to build a strong foundation for our lives that doesn't depend on the popularity of a TV series or trends at the newsstand.

We all had careers before we became celebrities. And we've always known that we want to do more than a reality show. So we definitely have our Plan Bs. We're making the most of this time to create other businesses that will provide for us and our families even if you stop *Keeping Up* with us. (Not that we want you to, of course!)

5. Have fun!

If you can't enjoy yourself, what's the point? We're very fortunate to have exciting lives right now, and so of course we're savoring it all while we can! Totes magotes!* We've gotten to travel to so many places—London, France, Spain, Australia, Africa. A lot of times we'll bring our friends along so they can experience it with us.

It's nice to have someone do your hair and makeup and travel by car service and helicopter. Of course we like getting front-row seats at concerts and going backstage. And it's truly a thrill to meet singers and artists and politicians and other amazing people we admire.

We count our blessings and have a good time!

*KARDASHIONARY DEFINITION

TOTES, OR TOTES MAGOTES: That's just a way to say "totally." Sometimes we add "magotes" for no reason. To make it fun.

Derivation: "Totes magotes" was in that movie *I Love You, Man*, but it seems like we were saying it before then.

6. Try to stay awake.

Not to complain, but we are *so* tired. We've got so much going on at once—including stuff we have to do for those Plan B businesses we were talking about—that sleeping sometimes isn't an option.

We do sleep, of course, but usually not very much. We often have hair and makeup calls really early in the morning, sometimes before the sun's up. And the night before, we may be getting to bed after midnight because we had to host an event, or because our flight got in late. It's not unusual to have to fly across the country and make an appearance in New York City then leave several hours later and fly back to L.A.—all in the same day. And then fly somewhere else the following morning. Sometimes we have to do a photo shoot every day of the week, and they usually last all day.

Like we said, every job has its downsides. So you just have to deal with crazy schedules and fight off fatigue and remember that it's a pretty great job, no matter what.

QUEEN OF THE POWER NAPS

Kim: I yawn a lot. All the time. I have a really weird yawn, and a different yawn when I'm really tired, like about to pass out.

When I'm at a shoot and everyone breaks for lunch, I'll just go and have half a nap. I can sleep

WANGO TANGO

We all did Wango Tango one year, which is a daylong concert held every year in L.A. People like Lady Gaga were performing and there were thousands and thousands of people in the audience. Ryan Seacrest was hosting so he had the three of us and Kylie and Kendall and Rob all walk onstage, and he introduced us. It was dark and everyone was taking pictures and when you looked out it was like seeing nothing but twinkling stars. And everyone was screaming. They would have screamed if anyone, even a dog, had walked onstage. It wasn't about us. But it was so cool to see that, because we're not performers. Singers get to experience that all the time. They must feel like they rule the world!

anywhere, and even a few minutes rejuvenates me.

One weekend I had several events in Las Vegas. So the night before I left I had a spray tan at midnight, went to bed at one, and then left early in the morning. I got to my hotel and right away went into hair and makeup for three hours. I ordered room service so I could eat at the same time.

I went to the first event, came back, changed really quickly and had to head down to a dinner. I got full before the main course, and it was already 11:30—and I still had another event to go to after dinner. So I excused myself from the table. I went back up to my room and took a nap while everyone else was eating their main course. I set an alarm for fifteen minutes, napped, went back down, met everyone, and headed to another event at a nightclub. Everyone just thought I'd gone to the bathroom.

The ability to power nap is so valuable, I wish I could tell you how to do it. But I'm afraid you either have it or you don't. I do need a dark room, or an eye mask on, but then I just close my eyes and I'm out. Some lucky people like me can do it, but not everyone can. Sorry.

THE LEADER OF THE FREE WORLD MANAGES TO BE POLITE!

Khloé: I used to be out with Kim when she was famous, more famous than Kourtney and me. Sometimes people would be introduced to me and they would not even look at me. I would say, "Hi, I'm Khloé," and they'd say, "Nice to meet you" without ever taking their eyes off Kim! Then if they went to shake my hand later or something, I wouldn't. I'd just say, "Never mind." You know, I'm a person, too! So now if I'm out with a friend and people do the same thing to her, I call them on it. I say, "Excuse me! You should look her in the eyes when you say hi to her."

It's ridiculous, especially when you think that the actual President of the United States has no trouble being sincere and friendly to everyone in the room. After the Lakers—the L.A. Lakers basketball team if I have to explain—won the NBA championship they got invited to go meet the President. And because I was the wife of a Laker, I got to go, too. Though Lamar only told me three days before, leaving me no time to figure out what to wear or anything. Men just don't get it.

Anyway, when we got to the White House, they asked me if I needed security. I mean, I'm not high maintenance anyway but are you kidding? We're in the White House, for God's sake.

I went crazy with emotion being there. The President was laughing and funny and such a sweet, genuine guy. So engaging. When he shakes your hand you feel like he's your best friend. Which is the point of my story. Hello!

He asked Lamar, "How do you like being married?" And Lamar was like, "I love it." So Obama said, "You better say that, she's watching you!" I was just so floored and flattered that the President knew who I was.

FANTASTIC

Kim: I love my fans, and I go out of my way to reach out to them. I know what it's like. I'm a fan, too. I really, really like Jennifer Lopez. I think she is so beautiful and has such great style. And I identified with her curves. She made me think it was sexy to have a big booty. One time I had just pulled into the Beverly Hills Hotel, and got out of the car, and I see her walking down the stairs toward the valet. My best friend Allison was with me and she said, "What's wrong with you?" Because I was literally shaking. I said, "Oh my God. I'm going to faint. Jennifer Lopez is right there!"

Allison used to manage her, so she said, "I'll introduce you." And I said, "No no no! I don't want to meet her!" I was too nervous, and what if she turned out to be different than I hoped? But then she came up and said hi to Allison and introduced herself to me. And she couldn't have been nicer. It made me like her even more.

After that I'd run into her at the gym and since then I've gotten to know her. She's been so amazing to me that it makes me like her even more.

I'm inspired by her. Some celebs go to events and always sit in the VIP section and never leave. I like to go out in the crowd and take pictures of everyone and get their cameras and snap away. One time in Las Vegas right after our fashion line came out, I saw literally five girls wearing outfits from the line. I was so excited and waving at them, wanting them to come talk to me. I like being myself; I don't want to be unapproachable.

Kourtney:

When I first started getting recognized, I would hear someone calling from across the street, "Hey, Kourt!" And I would think, who is that? Do I know them from college? And then I'd realize they knew me from the show. Even now when I hear my name like that I think for a split second it must be one of my friends.

Ninety-nine percent of the people who come up to us are really nice. They say, "Oh, we love your show," or "We relate to you so much." But there's the occasional person . . .

Like this time in Beverly Hills, back when I was pregnant with Mason, Scott and I had just been to the gynecologist and there was a lady with a cute little girl. I was waving at the little girl, being friendly. The lady comes up to us and starts telling us how disgusting we are for bringing a child into the world without being married. And here I am nine months pregnant and just thinking how cute the little girl is. Scott got mad. He was telling her, "Don't yell at my pregnant girlfriend!" But I told him it's not worth getting upset over.

Then once Khloé and I were walking down the street in Miami and some guy walked by and says, "Where's the pretty sister?" We laughed and just kept going. And we decided that he looked like a troll.

I love meeting fans, but there is a time and a place and a way to go about it. I was in my store one day, working in the back, on a conference call. I could hear this woman out

EVEN NOW WHEN I HEAR MY NAME LIKE THAT I THINK FOR A SPLIT SECOND IT MUST BE ONE OF MY FRIENDS.

front keep insisting that I come out right now and take a picture with her kids. I would have loved to do it, and I even signed things for them, but I was on a conference call. She got very rude.

But most people are really great.

Khloé: I love my fans! Once in a while, though, I do feel some guidance is required when it comes to approaching a celeb. First of all, please, don't ask us something while we have food in our mouths. And please don't take a picture without our permission. Once I was sitting on a plane reading something and three girls go walking by. I guess they had a video camera because they go, "Khloé!" I looked up and they said, "Hi! You're on our video camera!" That's just rude. Kourtney was at the gym once, and you know the kind of weird faces you make when you're working out? Well someone had her camera phone right in Kourtney's face taking a picture. So Kourtney grabbed the phone and erased the picture.

PLEASE DON'T TAKE A PICTURE WITHOUT OUR PERMISSION.

Usually people are wonderful, though. One of my favorite fan encounters was at the radio station in Miami where I was working. The cutest little girl came in, five years old. I said to her, "How did you get to be so pretty?" And she said, "I just did one day." So adorable. Then she said, "I never saw a real star before." I'm like, "Who's the star?" She said, "You!" I didn't realize she was talking about me. Who would even think a five-year-old would be watching our show?

I'm so appreciative when people want to meet me. It does really bug me, though, when somebody comes up and says, "I know you hate this, but . . . " Then they ask to take a picture or have me sign something. It puts me on the defensive. I want to say, "Well, if I hate this, then why are you asking me?" I love taking a picture or signing, but just be yourself and come out and ask.

And you don't have to say, "I'm your biggest fan!" You wouldn't believe how many people say, "Oh, Kourtney, I love you, I'm your biggest fan!" and then I say, "Well, obviously you're not my biggest fan, because I'm not Kourtney." It happens to Kourtney, too, they call her Khloé. It doesn't make us mad or anything. In fact, they usually feel bad about it, so we try to make them feel better. "It's okay, we're sisters," I say. But you don't have to try to be our biggest fan. We're just honored that you like us.

PAPARAZZI, PRESS, AND PERKS

12

When you're a celebrity, there are some annoyances you just have to get used to—such as being photographed when you really don't want to be photographed, and having to deal with people saying things in magazines and online that just aren't true . . . and . . . Haters!

You don't have to be a celebrity to encounter haters. You may have met up with some haters in your life, too. Ours are maybe just a little more public about it.

Come to think of it, you may know what it's like when someone spreads a false rumor about you, too, or posts something mean about you online.

Okay, so let's just say you can relate to most of this, though hopefully you've managed to avoid the paparazzi so far.

The key to handling these nuisances is to:

1. Accept them. You cannot make them go away, and it's best to make peace with that fact.

2. Control what you can. We don't hate the paparazzi or the press. Not at all! (In fact, we don't even hate the haters.)

We recognized a long time ago that the paparazzi were just trying to do their job. So we're usually nice to them. Most of the time if you smile and let them have a picture of you, they're happy and they'll go away. And you might as well smile because you don't want to see some picture of yourself everywhere scowling and looking like Cruella de Vil.

Same with the press. We're grateful when they give us attention that helps our show or promotes our products. And it's nice to have them shoot major events in our lives like Khloé's wedding. So we cooperate with the media when we can.

But that brings us to the third essential step:

3. Ignore them if you have to.

Look, people are going to do what they're going to do, and that includes photographers and magazine editors and people who insult you on the Internet. If you can't control it, then you just have to decide that you won't let it bother you.

Of course, all of this is easier said than done.

The problem with paparazzi is you never know where they're lurking. If you go out to public events, of course photographers are going to be there, so you can prepare yourself. It's when you don't expect them that they can be a pain—and potentially damaging to your ego. You don't know what angle they might be shooting from, so if you're on the beach in a bikini and someone with a camera shows up, your first thought is, "I better suck it in!"

Sometimes they can be invasive, too. When we're at the hotel where we shoot *Kourtney and Khloé Take Miami* we don't lay out in the sun at the pool because paparazzi go to the top of hotels nearby and take pictures with long lenses. Even if we're out on our own balcony, we know they might be getting shots. If we just want to do a vacation kind of thing and be alone and relax, it's like we have to go to Bora Bora, or at least a private house somewhere. Oh well. There are worse things in life.

Same thing with stuff that's reported about us. It can hurt when you see the cover of a celebrity weekly screaming out some horrible thing about you that's totally made up. Especially if it's very personal and mean. Or on the Internet, where anyone can trash you and it goes around the world in, like, a nanosecond. At first we used to read all the crazy things that people said about us. Occasionally we would even get upset at each other for something we read online quoting one of us. But then when we actually talked to one another, we would find out that it had all been taken out of context.

> NOT EVERYONE IS GOING TO LIKE US, AND THERE ARE ALWAYS GOING TO BE A FEW PEOPLE WHO MAKE AN ISSUE OF IT. YOU CAN'T MAKE EVERYONE HAPPY, YOU JUST HAVE TO TRY TO MAKE YOURSELF HAPPY.

Now we try to take it all in stride. If people say, "You guys aren't talented, why should you have all this success?" we just figure, well, if you don't think we're talented, that's okay, but at least we hope you see that we've worked hard to be successful.

Not everyone is going to like us, and there are always going to be a few people who make an issue of it. You can't make everyone happy, you just have to try to make yourself happy. If we don't let ourselves be drawn into an argument and just keep on being ourselves, maybe they'll even change their minds. It's happened before. People who were totally down on all Kardashians met us and said, "Hey, you're actually nice."

If we didn't shrug off the negativity, we'd be freaked out all the time.

Even though we do try to stay away from toxic places online, it is great after someone posts something hateful about us, and all these other people come on and say, "How dare you? They're wonderful! We love them!"

The feeling is mutual, dolls!

CREATIVE WRITING

Kourtney: It's so ridiculous what you see in the press sometimes that you can't take it seriously. One time I read that a guy I'd never even kissed was my baby's father. That one really got under my skin. Where do they get this stuff? I am usually great at brushing all of the stories off. I am strong and confident in who I am and what the truth is. But when it comes to my baby, that's another story. That's when I get angry. Same goes for the

paparazzi. New York paps are the best; they stay far away, get their shots, don't say a word to me, and leave me alone. There are a few L.A. paps that act almost like stalkers. And when I am with Mason I get super protective. If they keep at a distance and don't talk to me, I'm cool. Once they start with the sarcastic remarks and stand too close to me or my son, I lose it.

DON'T SHOOT!

Kim: I have a love-hate relationship with the paparazzi. I always try to be gracious. There's a fine line, though, of maintaining your privacy. It's hard when dating and trying to keep things private.

Sometimes paparazzi show up when you least expect it, though. So I do like to look at least a little bit cute when I go out. And have sunglasses.

FLY GiRLS

We have to travel a lot these days—mostly, it seems, we go to Las Vegas, Miami, and New York—so we end up spending a lot of time in airports.

KIM: Yes! It's so funny, last week I was at the airport, and I hadn't seen Khloé in at least five days. So someone says to me, "I just saw your sister, here at the airport." I said, "Where?"

KHLOÉ: So they found me, and Kim and I met and we got to spend a little time together at the airport between flights.

KIM: I love to fly.

KHLOÉ: I hate to fly.

KOURTNEY: I don't mind flying, but it's definitely harder with a baby.

KHLOÉ: I'm ADD anyway so being cooped up in that little space just drives me nuts. I have to go to sleep or else I get too restless.

Anyway, as we were saying, even though we live in Los Angeles, we're in Las Vegas, Miami, and New York a lot. Sometimes they feel like our homes-away-from-home. So we thought we'd give you some really quick insider travel tips on all three fab cities.

LAS VEGAS

Kim: I love Vegas. It's complete mayhem from the moment we get off the plane. It's great to fly there but it doesn't really matter how you get there. Driving's good, too.

I would say the best thing to do is go lay out by the pool all day, for two days. And then spend one day shopping. Caesar's Palace has amazing stores.

At night, Tao nightclub is fabulous. It's at the Venetian Hotel. And we go to Pure, too, at Caesar. That's where I danced with the Pussycat Dolls.

MIAMI

Khloé: Honey, Miami is all about the beaches. No matter what time of year it is, it's great to go to Miami for the beach, start to finish.

STK in Miami is amazing, much more fun than the one in L.A. It's a steakhouse that plays music like a nightclub. Another steakhouse, Prime One Twelve, is divine. And DeVito restaurant is a good place to bring a friend, it's very entertaining. Yes, it is owned by Danny DeVito.

The Fontainebleau is the perfect place to stay. The hotel used to be big a long time ago in the Rat Pack era, with Marilyn Monroe and all that. Then it was totally over for a while, but now they've fixed it up and it's really hot again. It's definitely the place to see and be seen.

Just hanging out at the pool during the day is really fun. And there are a ton of incredible restaurants there. What's the one we always go to? The Hakassan. And then you can go to one of the nightclubs right there at the hotel. You never have to leave so you don't have to worry about driving.

For shopping, go to Collins Avenue. It has all these chic boutiques, and Dash Miami, of course, is one block over on Washington.

NEW YORK

Kourtney: We used to make a lot of trips to New York for Dash and I've gone a lot with Scott, because that's where he's from. New York has so much culture, so much energy. It is the city that never sleeps. There is always something to do in NYC, like go to a museum or take a stroll through Central Park. I go to a lot of museums in New York; they're more accessible than those in L.A. and there seems to be more of them.

And oh the shopping! There is no better shopping in America than in New York City. I would have to say New York also has the best food hands down. The best Italian, Chinese, pizza, bagels, take out . . . they have it all. We love Italian, so we like to go to Bar Pitti and Serafina or to eat outside at Da Silvano. My sisters and I like to go to Cipriani and have a Bellini, a drink made with peach puree and Italian sparkling wine.

For Chinese there's Philippe on East Sixtieth Street. Fred, the restaurant at Barneys department store is good, too, and it's very convenient when you're shopping.

On our sisterly trips for Dash, we used to go clubbing until five in the morning and go to our appointments at 9 A.M. But not one inch of me has any desire to go to a nightclub these days.

13

LIVE! FROM HAIR AND MAKEUP!

"We're girls' girls, we all just want to be groomed."

—Khloé

We all love to get dressed up. We all love makeup and primping.

So naturally we love h&m. That's short for hair and makeup, which is what we have to do at least several times a week.

Hair and makeup is when we sit and have our hair done and our makeup applied before filming our shows or doing a photo shoot. You need special makeup for the cameras, heavier than we wear in our daily lives, and it takes a long time to get it all on our faces so that it will look just right and last all day. And we have to have hairstyles that withstand the hot lights and the long days, though we do have our stylists nearby through the day to do touchups during shoots.

And of course we have to look fabulous. Luckily, our stylists not only work their magic on the outside, they also do a good job of making us feel great, too. They're very supportive and know that part of looking good on camera is feeling confident about your appearance. That's true even when you're off camera, but cameras can catch you at a weird angle or magnify the things you'd rather minimize.

If we're filming our shows, we wear our own clothes, but if we're having our pictures taken, we might also have wardrobe stylists there with racks full of clothes and tons of shoes and jewelry all laid out. It's great, you go through the racks saying, "I like this one," and "What about this one?" and you try things on and who wouldn't love it?

Usually there are two hair and makeup stylists, so we take turns sitting in their chairs for the different phases of the whole grooming production. It's always nice to have someone transforming you into this glam creature while you just sit there. It's good to have an expert on board, you know? And you get to know your h&m stylists really well, too, so it's like having someone you can confide in, gossip with, and look to for advice and opinions about different things. Like you know, if you go to the hair salon and get to be buddies with your stylist, they become kind of a special friend you'll tell secrets to that you might not tell anyone else. That's what our hair and makeup stylists are like, except we see them all the time, without makeup, when we just get up in the morning. They *so* know us. We love our glam squad!

For sure it's nice to have the attention, but the process of getting all three of us done does take hours. So we often have to get up really early in the morning in order to make our h&m call. Truthfully, we would love to just spend those hours still asleep in bed. But we know we can't. So we use that time to get other things done, both when we're in the chair and when we cycle out of it.

In fact, guess what? We're writing this whole chapter while we're in h&m! As we speak!! We're in the penthouse where we stay when we're filming *Kourtney and Khloé Take Miami*. We've got blow-dryers going and two tall director's chairs set around the dining room table, which is covered with makeup and brushes and all sorts of grooming tools. None of us are dressed yet, as in dressed for the day.

KIM: I'm wearing a short robe. I had the first call this morning at 6:00.

KOURTNEY: I'm in the tank and shorts I slept in. Mason is still asleep. He's like his dad, he sleeps late.

KHLOÉ: And I'm in a tank and my pajama bottoms. I didn't have to be here until 7:30. Yay!

KIM: I am so exhausted. I didn't get in until almost two last night. I'm going to just close my eyes a bit here in the chair.

KOURTNEY: Kim, do you want me to make you some steel-cut oatmeal? I'm making it for like ten people already.

KIM: Can I have some later? Thanks.

KHLOÉ: What does that mean, steel-cut?

KOURTNEY: They're the real oats, not instant. They're better for you.

KHLOÉ: Kourt, how much do you get paid every time you say something about them?

KOURTNEY: Very funny.

KIM: Hey, Khloé, did you give me back my black top? My black Alexander Wang T-shirt?

KHLOÉ: I gave it back to you forever ago. I dry-cleaned it and gave it back to you on my hotel hanger.

KIM: I never got it.

KHLOÉ: Kim, I gave it to you.

KIM: I never got it.

KHLOÉ: I brought it to you!

KIM: I never got it.

KHLOÉ: Okay, I'll buy you whatever.

KIM: My makeup was amazing yesterday! It lasted forever. Even if I scratched my face with a big nail it would have stayed on. And I laid out in the sun. It was flawless when I got up and went straight to the Alicia Keys concert. I can't believe how cement it was. I think I need a little more blush here now, though. I feel like my face has been looking so pale and washed out, like it needs some color.

KOURTNEY: You know what we should do? One night we should all do each other's makeup, and then go out. And we have to wear the makeup we put on each other.

KIM: Kourtney, is Mom still around today?

KOURTNEY: Yeah, but I don't know what she's doing today. I don't know if she's coming here or what.

KHLOÉ: Happy birthday, Lady Gaga!

KOURTNEY: What?

KHLOÉ: It's her birthday today!

KIM: My whole body is sticky, you guys!

KOURTNEY: Why?

KIM: I sprayed this SPF on it, see?

KHLOÉ: Let me touch it . . . You are not sticky!

KIM: It feels smooth but if I put on my shirt, see how it sticks to me?

While we're getting all dolled for filming today, we've got the E! crew setting up lights and stuff in the apartment and people are coming in and out.

We're so used to doing other things while we're in hair and makeup that it's like second nature for us now. We also do hair and makeup before a talk show or something. They usually tape in the afternoon or early evening, so on those days we go into h&m there at the studio at a much more civilized hour than this. Though this really isn't too bad; we've had to get up much earlier before.

We can actually get a lot done during h&m. We can talk on the phone and catch up with friends. See what's happening on the blogs. We do a lot of texting. Sometimes no one is saying anything at all, it's complete silence, but all our thumbs are moving. And this is a good time to get business done, too. Sometimes we even meet with people.

KOURTNEY: Kim, I want to show you really quick these dresses I'm looking at to get for the store. Here, they're on my laptop.

KIM: I like that one.

KOURTNEY: Yeah, Khloé liked this other one, too. So should we get these both? Which colors?

KIM: How about every color except the green and the black?

KOURTNEY: Okay. Mason's up, I need to feed him now. Hi, Munchkin!

KIM: You know, S----- Twittered something about me again. She's really being rude. Should I say something to her?

KHLOÉ: No, it's cooler if you just ignore her.

KIM: Oh, I have to show you this picture. No, wait, it's on my other phone. Could you get it for me, Khloé?

KHLOÉ: Here you go.

KIM: Look, isn't this great? Should I Twitter it?

KOURTNEY: Why not? Hey, you guys want to know what Kim said to me the other day, by the way? I was standing there with my shirt off, and Kim said, "Are you really freaking out about your stomach?" I was like, "What about my stomach?" And she said it wasn't the same as it was, like it must be so weird to have your stomach get so big when you're pregnant and then not go back.

KIM: No, I was not saying that.

KOURTNEY: Yes, you were saying my stomach's not the same. I don't care. It was funny. I'm over it now.

KIM: No, you look ten times better now than I do and you had a baby!

KOURTNEY: That is definitely not true. Liar!

Hair and makeup is a perfect time to talk about clothes and girly things and what's happening with other celebrities. Hey, we're interested just like you! And we definitely like to get advice from each other and help each other out. Like if Kim is having a wardrobe moment, when she doesn't like anything she tries on, one of the other two of us will say, "Here, take what I'm wearing. I'll change."

KIM: So how does this look?

KHLOÉ: I like the jeans.

KIM: Do you think nude shoes with it?

KOURTNEY: Yeah, nude shoes.

KIM: Can I borrow that bag of yours, Kourtney?

KOURTNEY: Sure.

KHLOÉ: That reminds me, you two were supposed to be back from lunch yesterday like two hours before you finally got here.

KOURTNEY: There's that huge music conference in town, the traffic was a nightmare.

KHLOÉ: Yeah, yeah. Kim, tomorrow I don't have to film. I want to work out and get some sun. I'm going to go all day without makeup, don't you think?

KIM: Yes, you should definitely let your skin breathe. And maybe do that mask.

KHLOÉ: Look, Mason and I are dancing!

KOURTNEY: Mason is like, I have absolutely no idea what is going on.

KHLOÉ: They already want to take our order for lunch. I'm going to order a Diet Coke with. And don't say anything, Kourtney!

KOURTNEY: It's not very good for you.

KHLOÉ: Listen, honey, ya gotta live a little!

KIM: Khloé, if you're worried about getting done so you can go home this weekend, I can stay an extra day. You can get your stuff done first, so . . .

KHLOÉ: So I don't throw a fit? Thank you! I made Easter baskets for everyone right before I left, but don't tell them, they don't know.

KOURTNEY: Okay, we're done with my hair now, right? Khloé, it's your turn. So I guess I'm ready for makeup.

KIM: You two didn't get to have a roller fight like you did the other day.

KHLOÉ: No, the timing was off. Kourtney's hair was already out of rollers by the time mine was in.

KOURTNEY: The crew is telling us to hurry up.

KHLOÉ: Let's get ready for some reality!

Hair and makeup does give us a chance to catch up with each other. We'd still rather sleep in, but it's always nice to have sister time.

GETTING
GORGEOUS

Kim: I'm all about being clean. I believe that's the foundation of beauty. Feeling confident is based on good grooming.

First of all, I always try to wash my face and brush my teeth before I go to bed. If I'm too tired and just go to bed I feel so gross when I wake up the next day.

My mom believes you should always use products from the same skin care line on your face. She thinks it ruins your skin if you're not consistent. We created PerfectSkin, our own skin care line, so we'd have the best of the best. And she taught us to exfoliate, too. My skin tends to be dry, so I always have to use products that add moisture.

When I'm making up myself, I put on a primer first. I think it's really important. Smashbox makes a good primer. For eyeliner I like MAC liquid eyeliner in black. It's really, really black and it just glides on. I like to use a liquid lifting concealer under my eyes either from Christian Dior or Make Up For Ever. And I always have translucent powder with me for touch-ups. You can get a good translucent powder from the Laura Mercier line, Shisheido, or Bobbi Brown.

For nails, I *love love love* all of Sally Hansen's products. I also like shampoos by Finesse and Herbal Essence, and Suave mousse.

Khloé: My sisters taught me how to put on makeup. They actually went to a makeup class so they had the right to teach me! I always do my own mascara, even when I'm getting hair and makeup. I only use Lancome, either Hypnose or Drama. And I use Chanel waterproof eyeliner pencil or MAC or Stila, because they're so black. When I'm doing my own makeup I like to use Chanel foundation because it's really easy to apply. They have a liquid kind and a palette; the liquid is light and gives you a shade of color. The other is thicker, for when you want more coverage. Both of them go on really smoothly with no streaking.

I use two body lotions (and now Lamar does, too). One is by La Mer, which is very expensive, but the other is something I order online. My mom always used this certain type of lotion on me since I was a baby so now I get it from Homebody.com, customized with elderflower and china rain scents. It reminds me of my childhood.

FEELING CONFIDENT IS BASED ON GOOD GROOMING.

For my fragrance I am wearing a ton of sample mixtures because Lamar and I are in the process of creating our own unisex fragrance.

Some things I just have to have at all times in my bathroom. They're beauty staples. For instance, Vaseline is an amazing product. About once a week I slather it onto my feet and put socks on. I wear them for about an hour and, ta-da! My feet are as smooth as a baby's bottom. And of course the PerfectSkin products keep my skin clear and radiant.

Whenever I get a break from photo shoots and have time to myself, I don't wash my hair for three days. It feels so good to let it be. I wear extensions in my hair during the time that we're filming. They're just braided in. I had to wear extensions after the stress of my father's death made me lose my hair, so it's no big deal. I wore a full head weave for two and a half years while it was growing back. And then it was so much thinner than before, and not curly anymore. I take out the extensions when we're not filming. My suggestion if you want to get extensions is to spring for the very high-quality extensions and have someone do them who is really skilled at it. It will cost more but it'll be worth it.

I'm paranoid about having bad breath or body odor, even though I don't have either. I always carry deodorant in my purse. No particular brand. Every time I run out I get a different kind because they lose their effectiveness after a while.

One thing I always believe about beauty: Imperfection is beautiful.

> MY SUGGESTION IF YOU *WANT* TO GET EXTENSIONS IS TO SPRING FOR THE VERY HIGH-QUALITY EXTENSIONS AND HAVE SOMEONE DO THEM WHO IS REALLY SKILLED AT IT.

Kourtney: My beauty philosophy is that you always have to reevaluate things. It's so easy to get into a rut. You have to evolve.

I usually do it each time we start a new season of one of our shows. I'll go through the magazines and see what the trends are, and I'll decide, like, Okay, I'm going to wear this particular nail polish the whole season, and then I do, all the time. Though I've learned that you cannot have wet nail polish with a baby. So if I want to have my nails done, someone else has to take care of Mason until I'm dry.

You should always take a step back and look at yourself and think, how can I update things? You change, and so should your look. Like, there's this really shiny, sticky lipgloss Mom wears, and she wears it all the time. I say, you know, you can wear matte lips, too, that's also in style. You have to switch it up.

Recently I am so over wearing tons of makeup and tight dresses and big hair. I like to throw my hair in a ponytail and be done. Especially now that I have Mason.

When I was in the eighth grade our dad's fiancée Denise took me and Kim for makeup lessons. Denise is great, we love her. It was fun, and it did start teaching us about makeup. But it was heavy, heavy makeup and we were way too young for that. Now I look at Kylie and Kendall and think they are just twins of Kim and me back then. They have all these scrubs and skin products and this and that, and all they do is break you out. Simple skin care is the way to go.

> ### YOU SHOULD ALWAYS TAKE A STEP BACK AND LOOK AT YOURSELF AND THINK, HOW CAN I UPDATE THINGS?

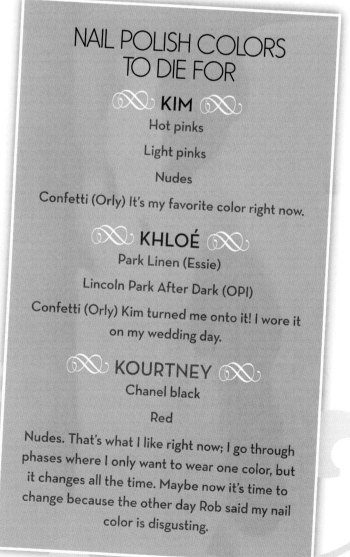

NAIL POLISH COLORS TO DIE FOR

⟳ KIM ⟳

Hot pinks

Light pinks

Nudes

Confetti (Orly) It's my favorite color right now.

⟳ KHLOÉ ⟳

Park Linen (Essie)

Lincoln Park After Dark (OPI)

Confetti (Orly) Kim turned me onto it! I wore it on my wedding day.

⟳ KOURTNEY ⟳

Chanel black

Red

Nudes. That's what I like right now; I go through phases where I only want to wear one color, but it changes all the time. Maybe now it's time to change because the other day Rob said my nail color is disgusting.

tweet
TWEET

Like hair and makeup, we couldn't live without our cells . . . and what they can do!

@kourtneykardash
we all twitter a lot. i guess the actual word is *tweet* but we usually just say *twitter*. i'd say kim does it the most and me the least.

@khloekardashian
i maybe twitter more than kim but she twitters the most pictures. she just loves 2 take photos of herself on her cellphone and twitter them.

@kimkardashian
thats unfair it makes me sound like i'm all into myself but thats not it. when i'm having fun i just love to share things with my fans.

@khloekardashian
at first it was hard keeping to 140 characters because you know dolls how i love 2 talk but once i got the hang of it it was fun. lol

@kourtneykardash
its a great way to communicate with a lot of people especially if you want to get something out there really fast.

@kimkardashian
and we follow people. i follow motivational people like @ihatequotes, which ironically has inspirational quotes.

@khloekardashian
the daily love is my favorite. it gives inspirational daily quotes about love and every day they have a theme. and rev run is really great.

@kimkardashian
i use twitter to stay on top of whats going on with kourtney and khloe sometimes when I havent seen them for a while.

@khloekardashian
we even talk 2 each other on it like i'll tweet kim and say i miss u how have you been?

@kourtneykardash
khloe and i can be kind of out there with our twitters like the other day we were asking everyone so do ants have genitalia?

@khloekardashian
well we really wanted 2 know. and we thought it was so funny like ants are so small and so we just wondered!

@kourtneykardash
and so then khloe and i were sending each other twitters about it and it was hilarious. its just fun to send funny stuff like that.

@kimkardashian
the two of u can send out twitters that i could never send, because if i said some of those things u do people would think i was crazy.

@khloekardashian
its just that we have different personalities that we R known for and so people expect me 2 be outrageous but U have to be the demure one.

@kourtneykardash
we can be rude because people know thats just us but if kim even says hi bitch they will think she's being mean even tho she's not.

@khloekardashian
thats why i think there R different twitter rules for different people. i can say anything and everything and no one cares.

@kimkardashian
but u have to be civil and its a good rule to be diplomatic. we forget how many people R out there and see it so u should always be aware.

@khloekardashian
when other so called celebs talk trash about kourtney or kim i get very protective and so mad and sometimes i lash back.

@kourtneykardash
and do u think its nice to hack into other peoples accounts like u two did to me the other day?

@khloekardashian
oh that was a joke get over yrself honey. pranks R fun like on april fools when nicole richie stole kims account and posted dirty msgs.

@kimkardashian
but u gave her my password khloe so she could. it was ok tho it was funny. but khloe u do steal everyones twitter.

@khloekardashian
don't be jealous just cuz i'm the fun one. just kidding! Lol!

14

PERSONAL BEST

Who wants a great body? Pretty much everyone.

Who thinks they have a great body? Pretty much no one.

One thing that we girls really have to get a handle on is being more accepting of our bodies.

We always like to look our best and we totally think that's a good thing to strive for. But obsessing over your weight and your "flaws" and basing your whole self-image on your appearance? Not so much. Besides, that kind of stress and panic will show on your face, which is not attractive. And did you know stress can make you gain weight? Not only does it make you eat more, but it also produces these hormones that have been scientifically linked to belly fat. Bible!

We've already told you about the struggles we went through when we were younger and unhappy with our bodies. Do as we say, not as we did: Don't go there!

Beauty comes in all shapes and sizes, and everybody has their own preferences. That's the naked truth. The three of us have three different body types. We can tone our bodies, shrink them, stretch them, whatever. But in the end, we'll still have the same basic bodies we were born with, even if they're firmer, slimmer, and more flexible bodies, which we're not knocking.

The sooner you accept your body, the sooner you can embrace it, and the sooner you'll be on your way to looking totally hot in your totally individual way. Trust us.

We all love to eat. And we all work out. We think our bodies are fit and attractive, but we're not slaves to certain numbers on a scale. We could never feel confidence in being unhealthy, and as you know, we're all about confidence.

If we decide to lose weight, we do it by eating more of the healthy things we like to eat and cutting back on some of the more indulgent treats that we love. But we don't stop enjoying ourselves. And we've never lost so much weight that we've gotten to the point of unhealthy skinniness. Doing extreme dieting or other stuff to make yourself that thin is very bad for you and can truly endanger your health. We've seen firsthand with people we've known how destructive it can be.

It's ironic. Sometimes after we've lost weight, we've found that some people actually prefer us the way we looked before. See what we mean? To each his own. Beautiful bodies are in the eye of the beholder—and in the heads of their owners.

BODY AFTER BABY

Kourtney: After I had Mason, I wasn't in any rush to lose the weight I gained during pregnancy. Breastfeeding takes a lot of the weight off, so I lost a lot of it easily, not changing anything. In fact, I never had cravings while I was pregnant, but when I was breastfeeding I craved sweets. And I'm normally not a sweets person, I go for things like chips with fat and salt. But sweets were all I wanted. My mom would come over and bring all these Christmas cookies and brownies and I would eat them all day long. And I still lost twenty pounds.

Then I went back to working out again. I really like to run, though lately my knees have been bothering me so I do the elliptical, too.

I have changed the way I eat some. Now I have breakfast every morning, which I think is good for your metabolism, and then throughout the day I make sure I eat something whenever I feel hungry. I'll have a cup of cherries,

or peanut butter with banana. And I've really gotten into nuts and dried fruit. Even though I lost the baby weight a long time ago, I'm still eating that way. For my meals, I eat whatever I want.

I definitely never deprive myself. If you asked me how often I indulge myself with a food splurge, I'd say every day. Absolutely. A cheeseburger with fries and a shake is always good. I also love DoubleStuf Oreos. And New York–style pizza with the thin crust. And I love having Mexican food and margaritas.

While I was pregnant, my butt got juicier, which I loved. But about three months or so after I had Mason I felt bad about my body for about a week. It was the only time in my whole life that I felt insecure about my body. I didn't realize that after you had a baby your stomach wouldn't just completely flatten out immediately. Especially after losing the baby weight. It was in Miami, I was like, wait, what's with my belly? But then I thought, who cares? I'm breastfeeding. I'm eating for two. Then I was past it.

My mom always tells me that I don't let Kourtney talk, so when we did Letterman (May 2010) I really tried to be quiet and let Kourt shine. She was amazing—such a pro! Then when I got offstage I had a phone call from Kris who was yelling at me for not speaking! LOL . . . I'm at a loss about how to please her. :) — *Khloé*

166

It, VARIES

Kim: I like to mix up my workouts! I use Gunnar Peterson as a trainer and he switches our workouts so we go from squats to lunges to weights. I also do Barry's Bootcamp, which is a great cardio workout. They have classes in L.A. and San Diego but you can also buy their DVDs.

After I work out I like to have a healthy smoothie that has peanut butter and bananas in it. Sometimes for breakfast I'll eat scrambled egg whites with tomatoes and mushrooms and turkey bacon. And for lunch I might have a salad or chicken, and usually the same kind of thing for dinner. If I'm going to treat myself, no question, I go for a cheeseburger and fries. But the artichoke dip at The Cheesecake

Factory is really yum, too. And I love homemade vanilla cake, you know, like birthday cake? I really don't drink except for a glass of dessert wine if I'm celebrating. A real danger for me is cookies-and-cream ice cream. Once I start it's hard to stop!

I tend to prefer my body when it's thinner, but even then, it's never actually thin, you know? And that's fine! I like myself curvy and I definitely don't ever deprive myself.

I knew a couple of girls in high school who were obsessed with their weight and had eating disorders. It was so weird. I just couldn't understand why you would do that to yourself. They would give me tips and tricks for losing weight and I'd listen, but then I'd say, "Wow, I just could never do that stuff."

I would hope that young girls see me and my sisters and realize that we're all different shapes and sizes and we feel totally comfortable with it. We like our bodies, and so should they.

Sweating off THE SWEETS

Khloé: I love sweets. I love desserts. Ice cream I'm crazy about. I love all the bad foods like macaroni and cheese. I just don't eat them all the time. And I like to work out.

I try to work out every day when I'm not filming. I have to go in the morning. If I ever say I'll do it later, it never happens, because I'm so exhausted. My body wants to do something every day—if not cardio, weights. It feels good, like I've accomplished something.

My favorite is boxing. I love to box with a passion. It gives you a workout from your toes to the top of your head and it's a huge stress reliever. You sweat so much it's like you've been in a sauna. I love to sweat when I work out.

Like I said before, I love food. I just try to eat the really fattening things in moderation. And I do drink, but same thing: It's fine as long as I don't go overboard. I like to enjoy myself.

I don't usually eat breakfast, though Lamar tries to make me. I'm just not hungry for breakfast. If I'm in a hotel I do like to order in something, like cottage cheese and fruit.

I have salads for lunch. I love salads, especially fruit salads, or salads with fruit in them. Like greens with mandarin oranges and grilled chicken. I prefer salads that I get in restaurants or for take-out because they come with so much more stuff than I can ever think to put in them myself.

After Lamar's games, we go out to eat or do take-out. We eat a variety of things, sometimes heavy, sometimes light. Often we go for Italian or

> I DON'T USUALLY EAT BREAKFAST, THOUGH LAMAR TRIES TO MAKE ME. I'M JUST NOT HUNGRY FOR BREAKFAST.

OUR FAVORITE INDULGENT TREATS

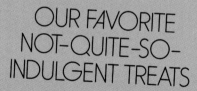

◄◄ KOURTNEY ►►

Double Stuf Oreos

cheeseburger, fries, and a shake

New York–style pizza

◄◄ KIM ►►

cookies-and-cream ice cream

homemade vanilla cake

cheeseburger and fries

◄◄ KHLOÉ ►►

ice cream

macaroni and cheese

honey wheat pretzels

OUR FAVORITE NOT-QUITE-SO-INDULGENT TREATS

◄◄ KOURTNEY ►►

avocado with lemon and sea salt

nuts and dried fruit

◄◄ KIM ►►

peanut butter and banana smoothies

◄◄ KHLOÉ ►►

peanut butter with apple

Chinese. We love MR CHOW but it's really expensive. Sometimes we do sushi. I eat a lot of chicken because I don't eat red meat. I never have since I was very little. I really don't know why I started that but now red meat doesn't even appeal to me.

For snacks I like to eat peanut butter with apples. I also adore these honey wheat pretzels. They are the best things ever. I know there's no nutrition to them whatsoever but I could just eat them all day long, all the time. I even keep them in my car.

I never weigh myself, ever. Numbers will send you to an early grave. It's too easy to let them mess with your head. Even when trainers ask if they can

weigh me, I say, okay, but I don't want to hear what it is and I don't want to look at it and I'd rather you not even do it. I go by how my clothes fit, and I don't buy by size, either, I buy what fits me. I don't care if it's a 6 or 10. If you're shoving yourself into a 6 that's too small, you're going to look fatter. On the other hand, if you think you can hide the extra poundage by wearing big, loose clothes, sorry, that also makes you look fatter.

But really, why be so hung up on it anyway?

When I was heavier, I never thought I was fat. I look at pictures of myself and I looked great. And I was confident. I was wearing really tight fitted dresses that most girls of that size maybe wouldn't wear, but I just felt that good. Even now when I gain weight, I don't think I'm fat. It's so easy to go the route of calling yourself fat and then, hey, why not have another cookie? I kind of looked at myself and said, "I may not be the skinniest person, but I'm making the best of this and I'm doing it healthy and I still feel beautiful." If someone doesn't think I'm pretty, that's okay. I'm fine. If you saw the show about me getting naked for my PETA shoot, you know I was really afraid of looking fat. But I did get over myself and now I have that poster hanging in my bathroom.

I NEVER WEIGH MYSELF, EVER. NUMBERS WILL SEND YOU TO AN EARLY GRAVE.

I'M OBSESSED WITH...

...STARBUCKS

Khloé: I love to get a Venti seven-pump no water chai latte. It normally comes with six pumps of tea but I need that little extra. When I'm in L.A. and not working, I get up at 8 a.m. and Malika brings me one.

...ROBES

Kim: I'm addicted to them. I feel disgusting when I get home and have to change out of my clothes. To me, robes are the epitome of comfort. I have ten of them, and they're all in light colors. I can't wear dark robes, or use dark towels either, or else I'll feel dirty. My sheets are light, too.

...STEEL-CUT OATMEAL

Kourtney: I don't know if I'd say I'm obsessed with it—I mean, I'm obsessed with Mason. But I am very into it. I never used to eat the first thing when I got up in the morning. I'd always wait until much later in the day. But I started doing it and now I get so excited for my breakfast! I use steel-cut oats, and I make it with light soy milk, and I have that every morning. It takes a little time to cook but I turn it on right away when I get up and leave it on the stove while I go do other things. It's so good, and good for you.

KOURTNEY'S STEEL-CUT OATMEAL

Steel-cut oats come in a can and they take longer to cook than instant oats. The soy milk gives the oatmeal more sweetness than regular milk.

◀◀ INGREDIENTS ▶▶

1/4 c. Irish steel-cut oats

1 c. light soy milk

1 tsp. manuka honey

◀◀ DIRECTIONS ▶▶

Put milk in a pan, stir in oats, and heat on high. Once the mixture begins getting thick, turn down the heat and simmer about 35 minutes.

FIT AND FEELING GREAT VERSUS SKINNY AND STARVING

◖ Don't give up the foods you love, just have them in moderation.

◖ Look for ways to make your treats more healthy. For example, when Khloé craves ice cream sometimes she'll have frozen yogurt instead.

◖ Don't deprive yourself. Eating is a good, healthy thing! Overeating is not. There's a difference.

◖ Eat when you're hungry, and stop when you're not. Ignoring hunger pangs can lead to pig-outs later on.

◖ Find out what kind of healthy snacks satisfy you. You may think of nuts as fattening, but they're full of good fat and high in protein and fiber. And they're totally yum. This goes for peanut butter, too. Nuts are high in calories so don't overdose on them, but don't fear them, either.

◖ Salads can be great meals, and really tasty. You can add all sorts of things to make them interesting and nutritious— veggies, fruits, nuts and seeds, cheese, meat and fish. Use your imagination and be creative. (Right, Khloé?)

◖ Make fitness, not weight loss per se, your goal. Strong muscles and flexibility and endurance will make you feel good and look good. Even if you'd like to lose a few pounds, concentrating on the health benefits of working out will make you more likely to keep it up and eat healthy, too. Plus, workouts reduce stress!

◖ Speaking of stress, remember, obsessing about your weight and being unhappy with your body only increases stress and poundage.

◖ Never, ever go to extremes with your diet or exercise routines. Anorexia and bulimia can kill you, so get help if you even have an inkling you're headed that way.

◖ Learn to love your body. It's beautiful and it deserves only the best.

Sometimes we have fun being interviewed all together. This was when *Nightline* was doing a segment on us in May of 2010. — *Kourtney*

15
STYLIN'

These are Christian Louboutin Safari pumps. I am obsessed with shoes—you should see my shoe closet! — *Khloé*

ashion. It's our middle name. It's what we live for. It's our drug.

We're exaggerating. But just the tiniest little bit.

We just can't get enough of clothes and shopping and accessorizing. It's all so fun, and so satisfying when you put together something that makes you feel chic and sexy and slim.

Of course clothes can make you look slimmer, if that's what you're looking for, or they can show off your arms or your butt or whatever feature you want to get noticed. We've all agreed that we want our bodies to be fit and strong, but if you know the secrets of style, your clothes can do wonders for your body, too.

Dressing to boost your fab quotient really comes down to two simple principles:

1. Choose the right things to wear. Certain clothes will make you look amazing, and others definitely won't. Whereas the stuff that sucks on you may look incredible on your friend—but then the clothes suited to you mysteriously add ten pounds to her figure. In other words, dress for your body type. This requires that you understand your body type and do some investigation.

2. Create your own individual style. Put together looks that reflect your personality and add little touches to outfits that will truly make them your own. A strong personal style makes you shine, and it will let you stand out in a whole crowd of fashionistas.

Don't think that if you dress for your body type you can only wear one or two different styles. Of course not! How could we ever expect you to limit yourself when we're constantly fighting over clothes and borrowing out of each other's closets? (Sometimes without permission.) A lot of things look good on all of us. But we'll wear them different ways, maybe add a belt or do a big chunky necklace or put leggings underneath. In fact, let's add a third principle of style:

3. Have fun. Use your imagination, don't be afraid to try things and mix it up. In style there really are no rules, except your own. (Hey, girl power even applies to fashion!) You'll see what we mean if we each explain how we approach our style challenges. We'll let Kourtney start, because among the three of us, she's known as the Freakin' Fashion Icon!

Kourtney:

I've always been super into clothes. I like a style that's effortlessly chic, not so perfectly done or matchy-matchy. Kind of more Bohemian. I'm very into comfort, especially now that I'm a mom. I shop at vintage stores a lot, and then I'll add or change stuff to update what I get. I often have to have things altered because I'm petite. It really pays to have a good tailor, no matter what your body type is. The right alterations can turn an okay fit into a fabulous fit.

Being short also means I usually have to wear shorter skirts and tops, to keep things in proportion. I can't really wear dresses to the knee. And I have to be careful about trends that are too overpowering. I've recently learned that when you have big breasts, a big loose shirt can make you look heavy.

I mix things up a lot. Like I'll wear something high-end with something from Zara or H&M that's cute. When my college friends and I first discovered Forever 21 stores, we were so excited. You could get really inexpensive clothes and then put them with more expensive shoes or handbags, and create your own unique look.

It's all in how you put it together to make it your own. Have confidence, have fun, and own it.

Kim:

My work as a stylist taught me some good style tricks, mostly about how to draw attention to your best features. When I styled my mom, for example, she didn't like her arms, so I dressed her with that in mind. With Khloé, I would try to show off her long legs. For myself, because I have a curvy figure, I dress to accentuate my waist by using a lot of belts, and I'm big on shape-wear.

I also learned that to master fashion you have to stay on top of things. I like to shop at different places, not just high-end stores, because I like to mix and match. I love Zara, and Forever 21 and H&M. You have to watch what they have in stock because trends sell out very quickly. Sometimes they'll only get a few of each piece. You need to keep coming back to check on what's happening. That pays off no matter where you're buying clothes.

I'd say my own style has evolved over the last few years or so. I used to be completely casual during the day with comfy clothes and flip-flops and then go to the opposite extreme at night and be super-dressy. I tended to wear really tight, short dresses with big hair and fab shoes. I still wear fab shoes but I don't wear things head-to-toe so much anymore, and try to go a little funkier. Maybe I'll put a vest over a dress, for example. And my day style is different from before. I don't think I even own sweats anymore. I'll wear jeans, maybe with leggings. I spend a lot of time lugging things through airports, so why not look cute while I'm doing it?

Khloé: Kim, you are just "it," whatever "it" is!

It's true we're all fashion-obsessed. I actually copied Kim's style a lot when I was young because Kourtney was away at college. Kim and I still have very similar tastes. We were walking by this shop window the other day and

We love our shoes! This was at a QuickTrim appearance; Khloé (on the left) is wearing Gucci Runway and I'm in Proenza Schouler. — *Kim*

Kim said, "Oh, I love that dress!" and I said, "Oh my God, I just bought it yesterday!"

My biggest challenge has always been figuring out what looks best on my body. I've discovered that can get a little tricky over time, because what flatters me most changes as I grow older. Maybe I become more comfortable in certain types of clothes, or lose weight, or my tastes shift a bit.

Minidresses and shorts look good on me because I have long legs. I don't care for my arms so much so I don't wear strapless tops or dresses. You have to wear what you feel comfortable in because then you'll look better, too.

I'm a high heels girl and always have been. I know I'm tall and they make me taller, but I don't care. I just love the sexiness of a high heel, so most of my stuff I wear with heels.

I don't think you should take yourself too seriously with clothes, or take yourself too seriously at all. Sometimes your idea of looking great is not going to correspond with someone else's. It's fun to surprise people and look different from them. Shocking people occasionally can be a high. But I have to keep in mind that wearing something in person is different than getting photographed. Certain wild color combinations might not show right in photos.

I know Kim and Kourtney love to accessorize with belts and trendy jewelry but I don't so much. I am very into diamonds, just diamonds. So I'll wear diamond earrings or diamond hoops and necklaces and of course my diamond ring. My sisters try to go the extra mile with fashion, but I guess I don't care that much.

Now we want to talk about your closet. What, you may ask, does your closet have to do with your clothes, besides being somewhere to put them? A lot!

First of all, yes, it's true, your clothes go into your closet, and that means that you're presumably dealing with a finite amount of space. Kim converted a whole bedroom of her new house into a closet with a beautiful chandelier and built-in shoe cubbies and a special section for her jewelry. It's huge, and it is totally to die for, but even she is dealing with finite space!

So you have to keep that in mind when you're building a wardrobe. You only have so much room, so you have to make the most of every bit of it. Which means you have to think hard about what you have, what you need, and how to be smart about adding pieces to it. Hint: think mix 'n' match!

For example, these are some of the basics we have at the core of our wardrobes that might be good for you:

- A black blazer, and one in cream if you have the money and space for it

- A little black dress

- A pair of skinny jeans, or "jeggings," which is a very annoying word for jeans that are like leggings

- Black leggings

- A pair of boyfriend jeans

- An amazing pair of black shorts

- A white button-down shirt

- A belt you can wear over everything

- Two pairs of black heels, one open-toe and one closed

- A pair of nude pumps, which are great for elongating the look of your leg

- A pair of thigh-high boots

- A pair of comfortable, yet stylish, flats

- A fabulous purse. This could be your big splurge!

Your basics may differ from ours, of course. Not everyone may be as into thigh-high boots as, say, Kim. But the point is that you should pay a lot of attention to your basics, and probably spend the most money on them. They're the bedrock of your wardrobe, so you want things that will be easy to pair with each other and with other things like tops and accessories. And you want them to last. So they should be classics—not trendy pieces. Go for the highest quality you can afford.

Now of course you want to have special going-out stuff in your wardrobe, too, so allot some room in your closet for a couple of killer outfits. Maybe one can be trendy and less expensive, the kind of thing you could let yourself buy once a season. And the other could be something fabulous and timeless that you look incredible in.

For the rest of your closet, you need to assess the space left over from your basics and your wow outfits and decide what extra pieces and accessories will add the most to your options. You want to aim for creating as many outfits as possible from the fewest possible pieces.

Think logically, and mathematically. If you have a blouse that will go with one pair of jeans, a pair of shorts, two blazers, and two pairs of shoes, you've got . . . well, it's too hard to do the math right now but it's obvious that you've automatically got a bunch of outfits right there just by putting that one blouse with different pieces in different combinations. And you can mix them up even more with accessories like jewelry and scarves. If you do it right, it's like a fun little puzzle that goes on forever!

YOU WANT TO AIM FOR CREATING AS MANY OUTFITS AS POSSIBLE FROM THE FEWEST POSSIBLE PIECES.

Accessorizing according to trends is a good way to keep things fresh without spending too much money. Say if necklaces are the thing one season, buy 'em up. You should be able to get some great ones inexpensively and they'll update your whole wardrobe.

We'll come back to your closet but first let's take a detour for shopping. (That's a detour we're always ready to make!) Seriously, remember you have to keep your closet in mind when you head out the door to go shopping. That's when you take all your hard-won knowledge and put it into action, in the exciting but very real world of retail.

DRESS TO IMPRESS CHECKLIST: SHOPPING

√ Don't be afraid to try on a lot of things. Then try on some more things. And some with a lot of different styles and fits and looks. Be ruthlessly honest with yourself, but don't approach it with the idea that nothing looks good on you. Have a positive attitude and you'll find what works.

√ Make your basics your first priority, but with basics and everything else, buy only things that you love. Don't be swayed by what's on sale or what everyone else is wearing. Go ahead and shop the sales, because you can save money that way. But if *you're* not totally sold on something, you'll regret it later.

√ If you find something to die for that you absolutely know will be a part of your wardrobe for years, consider getting it in different colors or even buying multiples, depending on what you can afford. But only if it's a style that will also endure for years. That means no trendy stuff.

√ We don't mean to belabor the point, but in general, don't buy trends except as we explained above. It's fun to pick up something of the moment if it's not too expensive. But mostly you should ask yourself, "Do I want this in my closet for a really long time? Do I want to devote precious space in my closet to this?"

√ Good fashionistas are frugalistas, too. We admit we probably spend a lot more money on clothes than some people, but we always look for ways to make the most of our purchases—and our closet space! Before we hand over that credit card, we think about what we already have in our closet. Does it duplicate something we've got? Will it go with a lot of other things? How many times will we wear it? You don't have to buy a whole new wardrobe each season if you focus on those essential, well-chosen basics that lay the foundation for lots of different looks. You can just add things that will multiply your outfits to the power of 10, or to the highest power you can.

√ Try to take someone along who can look at you from all angles and help you weigh your options. In fact, the best way to judge how something looks on you is to take a picture. You have to be brave. Sometimes you'll find out that from the back, a pair of pants doesn't drape right or you've got little belly rolls pooching out of your blouse. Or you could be pleasantly surprised to discover that a dress you like from the front turns into a totally amazing look from behind.

√ If you do take along a friendly shopping assistant, make sure it's not the kind of person who will egg you on to buy everything in the store!

Fabulous! You've got some great stuff that looks killer on you. It's time to go back to the closet. This is where organization comes in:

DRESS TO IMPRESS CHECKLIST: ORGANIZING YOUR CLOSET

√ **Determine a place for everything.**

√ **Arrange everything according to color, and within each color, order each piece from light to dark.**

√ **Don't have your shoes just tossed all over the floor, obviously, but don't put them in those hanging caddies, either. At least don't do it if they drive you as crazy as they do us. Some people like to keep their shoes in labeled boxes, but we like to have them in a place where you can see them, like in a shoe rack. Boots should always have boot fillers to keep them from crumpling.**

√ **Use dividers in drawers for jewelry.**

√ **Fold scarves neatly and put them in drawers.**

Everything in order? Okay, now this is where you can get really tricky. This will take some time, but it's totally worth it:

√ **Go through your closet and pull together outfits by figuring out which pieces you're going to put together.**

√ **Bring all the pieces out of the closet and hang them together somewhere so you can see them clearly.**

√ **Add belts and jewelry and other accessories.**

√ **Put the shoes you'll wear with the outfit beneath it.**

√ **Now take a picture of the outfit, and upload it into a folder on your computer marked either "Day" or "Night."**

Voilà! When you're totally in a rush, all you have to do is go to your computer, refer to your folders, choose an outfit, and you're out the door in a flash. After you've worn the outfit, you can delete the picture if you want and go make some new outfits from the pieces.

Okay, we're not done yet. Stocking and organizing your closet is important, but weeding it out matters just as much. Remember that finite space? You have to work within it, which means you must constantly edit your closet. It's simple: If you don't wear it, get rid of it. You can keep cool vintage pieces, but otherwise, you have to be heartless. If it's trendy and you'll never wear it again, it's out. If it doesn't suit your body anymore, out. If you meant to wear it lots of times but just never did, out. Make it a habit to clean out your closet often, and be tough.

Finally we come to the Number One most important style rule of all.

THE #1 RULE OF STYLE

We cannot emphasize enough that IT'S REALLY IMPORTANT TO TAKE GOOD CARE OF YOUR CLOTHES, SHOES, BAGS, AND EVERYTHING!!! It's wasteful to spend money on things you love and then treat them carelessly. They'll last you a really long time if you treat them with loving tenderness. Besides, fabulous clothes never die—they just get sold on eBay! If you treat yours right, you can sell them online and honestly say they're like new.

Who said fashion was easy? Looking good is a job, but it's such a fun one!

STRIKE A POSE

Looking good in photos isn't always easy.
Trust us! But we'll let you in on a few tricks:

Khloé:

1. Figure out the best angle for your face and use it.

2. Keep powder nearby to take down any shiny spots on your face.

3. Ignore what the photographer tells you to do.

4. Don't put your chin up. (How many chins do they want you to have?)

5. Try tilting your head down a bit while lengthening and straightening your neck.

6. Twist your body slightly (and naturally!) so you're about three-quarters facing the camera.

7. Put your hands on your waist to look smaller in the middle—unless you feel uncomfortable drawing attention to your middle.

8. Think happy thoughts and smile with your eyes.

9. Relax.

10. Make sure the photographer has Photoshop! LOL!

Kim:

1. Take the time to look in the mirror to see the way you look best.

2. Suck it in. LOL!

3. Have great posture.

4. Stick your booty out.

Kourtney:

1. Stand up straight.

2. Suck it all in.

3. Laugh!

Our photographer, Nick Saglimbeni, is very good at getting us to look just the way he wants for different shots. But we always check them out afterwards on his computer to make sure we like them, too. — *Kourtney*

I love getting all glammed up as a family. This occasion was the wedding of a really close friend of our family. — Khloé

16

BOYS

Boys! Boys! Boys! We love 'em!

On our shows you've seen us going through all sorts of dramas related to our love lives. Now we want to give you a peek at what goes on behind the scenes of the fights and the breakups and the makeups and even one wedding. We'll also confide in you about what we really think about men and marriage and love and relationships.

And after all that, how could we resist telling you all about the really special man in our life, Mason Dash Disick?

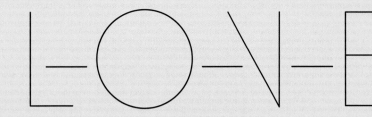

LOVE

When it comes to affairs of the heart, we each have our own individual personality. Just like we each have our own astrology sign. It's amazing how three sisters can be so different.

KOURTNEY: I'm the most calm and laid-back of all of us, the same way I am in the rest of my life.

KHLOÉ: Out of all of us, I'm the one who thinks most like a man. You know, I don't worry so much about pleasing random men.

KIM: But Khloé, you're kind of old-fashioned, too, because you believe in chemistry and fate.

KHLOÉ: I always say go with your heart, but make it 80 percent heart and 20 percent head. Because your head will keep you level but your heart will make you fly.

KOURTNEY: And Kim's in love with everyone.

KHLOÉ: Kim's in love with love.

KIM: It's true, I'm a hopeless romantic.

SINGLE AND SEXY

Before we get into all the love connection stuff, the first thing you should know is this: As much as we adore guys, as important as they are in our lives—*we're* more important.

That may sound weird, like we're selfish or self-absorbed. But that's not what we mean. It's just that you have to really love yourself before you can truly love anyone else. Being single helps you see that. We've all spent time out of relationships and we're totally glad that we did.

The single life is underrated. When you're on your own, you discover all this stuff about yourself that you never knew. It's good for you to have Me Me Me! time, because it's not only fun, it also helps you figure out what you truly want—from you and from other people.

Kourtney: Even when I first started dating Scott, I kept it casual for a while because I had just left a long relationship.

Kim: I talked about this earlier, how when I took a year to be single I gained so much confidence and broadened my horizons. And I had a blast. It was absolutely essential.

Our mom started having kids when she was very young. And then she had so many of them! She's always wanted us to hurry up and marry and have families of our own so we could be as happy as she's been. But we're a different generation, and we want to take each step as it comes. We don't want to be rushed.

Khloé got married between seasons three and four of *Keeping Up*, but before that when she wasn't with anyone Mom was feeling bad for her, pushing her to find someone. The other two of us were in relationships at the time and we wanted to see her happy with someone, too. It's natural for sisters to want to be in step with each other. But Khloé tried to explain that you don't need a man to be happy.

Khloé: When you're young you should be having a good time and finding out what you want in life. I was totally happy being single!

Relationships will happen when they're supposed to; you shouldn't push it. If you think you have to be married by a certain age and force it, sooner or later you'll be miserable and resentful.

I always got smarter about relationships when I was out of them. Some women go from boyfriend to boyfriend and they don't really have time to focus. If one person I dated didn't work out, I always took time to myself and tried to figure out what I learned from it. Everyone comes into your life for a reason. I would reflect on what drew me to that boy and what made me break up with him. Maybe it was because I didn't like the way he was treating me. So then with the next boy, I would know for sure that I wanted him to treat me differently.

When you're in the middle of a relationship, it's hard to work all this out. Your head is fuzzier than you realize. It's only when you step away from the environment that it becomes clear.

So bottom line, we like having men in our life but we believe it's really good to spend some time on your own, too. We may be crazy about boys, but we're not crazy.

Our family, however, *is* crazy.

DATE ONE OF US, DATE US ALL

If you're a Kardashian, you simply cannot have a relationship without everyone in the whole family being part of it. All of us are so close and involved in each other's lives that it's just impossible to avoid. We're very protective of each other.

We're grateful to have people around us who care and are always looking out for us. And we do spend so much time with each other and the rest of our family that a guy has to be able to enjoy that with us. If he can't, then he's not the right one.

But sometimes it can get out of control.

KIM: Kourtney and Khloé, you should talk about that.

KHLOÉ: Oh, you mean how Kourtney broke up with Scott and cried on my shoulder all that time and I was working so hard to help her, and then all of a sudden she's back together with him again? I couldn't believe it. I was just so upset.

KOURTNEY: It wasn't really a breakup.

KHLOÉ: Oh, it was a breakup. It was definitely a breakup! It really hurt me as a sister to have her drag me through the whole thing and then just turn around and . . . there he was again. I feel like it's my duty to protect Kourtney.

KOURTNEY: Khloé gets way too protective.

KHLOÉ: I was too involved. I just had to remove myself emotionally from that relationship to protect myself. I don't get like that with Kim. With Kim, she's so dramatic that, I don't want to say you don't listen to her, but you don't take it too seriously. Kim, you know what I mean, right?

KIM: I always get emotional, but Kourtney is usually so unemotional and okay with anything and everything.

KHLOÉ: Exactly. So I really took it to heart when she was in distress. You have to realize that when you end a relationship and lean on the people who care about you, they're going to take your side. Then if you get back together with that person you were screaming and sobbing about, it's going to be hard on the person who carried you through. I think the older we get, the more cautious we are about being so hands-on in each other's relationships.

KIM: Still, if we're having troubles we rely on each other 100 percent.

That's the thing about family—sometimes you can care so much that it hurts. Or so much that it makes you really angry. But it doesn't mean you stop caring. And even though we disagree with each other's choices sometimes, we support each other in the end.

Ultimately, we pretty much all want the same things out of a relationship, don't we?

Everyone in the family tries to come to Lamar's Lakers games. Kim gets really excited and LOUD! — *Khloé*

GOTTA HAVE IT

We each have our own ideas about the kind of guy we like physically or personality-wise. But when it comes down to truly letting some-one into our lives, we agree there are some definite necessities:

1. **He has to make us laugh.**

   No way we're going to spend time with someone without a sense of humor and the ability to entertain us. Life is too short not to have fun!

2. **He should be someone we're genuinely friends with.**

   By that we mean there has to be more than just sexual attraction. We have to be able to talk to him and count on him. If you're going to be with someone forever—and that's the goal, right?—then the relationship needs a lasting foundation that will keep things solid through the ups and downs of love that are inevitable.

3. **We have to be totally comfortable with him.**

   We think one good test of a relationship is whether the two of you can be perfectly happy just being together at home doing absolutely nothing— no TV, no phone, no computer. (Though we admit we have a hard time completely ignoring our phones and BlackBerrys.)

4. **He has to be cool with our careers and all the stuff that goes with them.**

   For a guy to be part of our lives, he has to be on our wavelength and not need babysitting. He should be at ease and carry himself well. That doesn't mean the guys we're with have to be famous. But they do have to be motivated and goal-oriented and adaptable.

5. **He MUST respect us and treat us right!**

   Exactly what that means may be different for each of us—and each of you, too. But you should never accept less than what you need, just to keep a relationship together. That can be a hard lesson to learn—we've all been there, when we really like someone and we bend ourselves a little to please him, and lower our standards a little bit to keep him around, and then maybe lower them some more.

Dude, don't do it!

We're not advising you to keep this long list of precise requirements a guy must meet before you'll even take a second look. Like, he has to be six foot two with green eyes, make x amount of money, drive a certain kind of car, have an IQ of 190, and play three sports, one at the semi-pro level or higher. That won't get you very far. Even if you get the outside thing just right you might be nowhere emotionally. Not only will you never find Mr. Perfect, you'll miss out on some great guy in the meantime.

But respect is one thing you should always be picky about, no matter what. When it comes to being treated well, insist on the very best.

Which leads us to an unavoidable topic that must be discussed.

CHEATING

One word: *unacceptable*!

Having said that, it's not like we haven't been in relationships where the guy fooled around and we put up with it for longer than we should have. Well, at least two of us have. Khloé says she's always left the second she found out.

And we do realize that every relationship is different. No one outside of a relationship knows exactly what goes on inside. In other words, we try not to judge. (And for the purposes of this conversation, we're leaving the whole issue of Kourtney and Scott out of it, because we don't want to get back on that big trauma between Kourtney and Khloé again.)

KIM: Right, you guys?

KOURTNEY: There was never any evidence that Scott cheated. Khloé and Scott are alike. They're both very stubborn.

KHLOÉ: I've washed my hands of the whole thing. But I did want to say, have you ever noticed, when you like a good-looking guy, and he turns out to be a complete jerk, he's not even good-looking anymore? It's like ooh, get away; you're not attracted to him at all.

A lot of times girls think, "How can I tell if my boyfriend is cheating?" People even ask Kim about it, because she's so good at breaking into people's voicemail and has all sorts of other little espionage tricks up her sleeve. (Sorry, she's not spilling.)

The real thing to ask is this: If you're worried about a guy cheating on you, why are you worried? Is he acting shady?* Do you feel shaky about the relationship? Are you paranoid?

If you're in a relationship and you feel you have to be checking all the time to make sure he's staying faithful . . . that's not the guy you want to be with.

Be careful, though, about listening to other people who may want to start rumors that aren't true. We know something about that.

*KARDASHIONARY DEFINITION

SHADY: We use that word a lot. And we've used it forever, at least ten years. It's a good all-purpose word for when something's up.

Derivation: We have no idea where it came from. Probably it was in a rap song and we stole it.

PUBLIC Affairs

When you're in the public eye and you're in a relationship, it seems like everyone (and by everyone, we mean the media) wants to know exactly where it's going at all times. Are you getting married? Or are you breaking up? Almost like it has to be one or the other.

Then if you decide to get married right away after meeting someone, everyone is like, Are you seriously getting married? What do you think you're doing getting married? Is it real? It'll never last!

And if you have a baby and you're not marrying the father, then, well, *Why aren't you getting married?* He must be breaking your heart!

Sometimes we want to say NOYB!

Most people just have to worry about their mother meddling in their love life, but we've got all sorts of people sticking their noses in all the time. If they don't really know much of anything, they just make up stories, like saying that your boyfriend is cheating on you. If the trust in your relationship isn't strong, that can put doubt in your mind.

Plus when you're a celebrity it is a little harder to trust someone, at least at first. You think, does this guy really like me for me?

Public scrutiny of your love life can be a drag, but like everything else, we've learned to live with it, and now we just try not to pay attention.

It does require a little bit of finesse, though. Particularly when it comes to breakups.

K-TIP FROM ALL OF US

HOW TO ATTRACT THE MAN OF YOUR DREAMS

◖ The more you know about yourself, the easier it is to know who to look for.

◖ The more confidence you have, the more drawn to you people will be.

◖ You pretty much get what you give. If you're a good person who's generous and loving and positive and thinks highly of herself, you're likely to attract a person who's generous and loving and positive and thinks highly of you, too!

◖ Look for someone whose core beliefs are compatible with your own.

◖ Above all, stay true to yourself.

SPLITS

If you do go through a breakup—and who hasn't?—it naturally puts you in a vulnerable place. Your feelings can be very tender for a while, especially in the first few weeks or so when you might be in shock or just going through the emotions of the separation.

We've found that it helps to give yourself time to lick your wounds in private, without the whole world knowing. As soon as there's a whiff of trouble in your relationship, everyone will be pouncing and digging for the whole story. It's tough.

Kim: After your first breakup in public, you learn how to handle it a little better. I try to be as open with my fans as I can, but it's good to keep it private for the first few weeks. I prefer to keep the media in the dark. I needed to deal with it first before everyone else started analyzing what went wrong.

Kourtney: Back when Scott and I broke up for six months, I kept it to myself for the first couple weeks. I mean, I told my close friends and my family, but no one else knew. It wasn't in the magazines. People didn't really find out until they saw it on an episode that aired later, and by then months had passed. I was over it.

Khloé: I don't think it's bad advice for anyone, really, to take time for themselves after a breakup. Like what I was saying before. And even when you're in a relationship, there's something to be said for maintaining your privacy. You don't have to tell people every little thing. It's so easy to vent about negative stuff. If your boyfriend is kissing your feet, you usually don't call your girlfriend all excited and say, "Oh my God, guess what he did for me!" But if he steps on your foot, you're like, "Oh my God, you know what he did to me?" If I'm having a bad day in my relationship, I try not to call people up about it, because in the long-term, it's really just more like a bad minute.

Yes, we definitely love guys, no matter how much confusion and irritation they cause in our lives. We all want to be loved, but we also want the kind of support and encouragement we've been lucky enough to have within our family. We want to have kids and houses full of laughter (and yelling). The perfect guy to help create a beautiful family is the one who already feels like family.

My typical day—at least when we're all in hair and makeup—starts with Mason kisses. I can't live without them! He's everything to me. — *Kim*

Mason Dash Disick,
19.5 inches, 7 pounds, 6 ounces,
entered the world on December 14, 2009

This was taken at a baby shower. I love it because it shows four generations of us—MJ, Kris, myself, and Mason! — *Khloé*

KHLOÉ: I love that Kourtney is a mom.

KIM: I love being an aunt. It's definitely showed me how hard moms work. When I babysit, I realize it's a lot harder than I thought.

KHLOÉ: When we're all together, Kim always wants to hold Mason. She cries if she doesn't get him.

KIM: It's funny because Kourtney didn't seem like someone who wanted to be a mom. She never babysat Kendall and Kylie. Whenever she talked to kids she wasn't all warm and fuzzy, like she wouldn't ever talk baby talk. She'd say, "No way! I'm not changing my voice for anyone!"

KOURTNEY: I wasn't the girl who grew up wanting to have a certain kind of wedding with the perfect dress followed by four kids. I was maybe a bit selfish. And I was a little scared of being pregnant and the whole process of delivering a child. Even when I was pregnant I couldn't stand to watch shows where a woman was giving birth. It freaked me out. I always said Kim would be my surrogate because she wanted lots of kids.

KIM: When I first walked in the delivery room and you were taking the epidural, you were shaking. But then you were totally calm throughout the whole thing. You never even screamed or cried. I cried, Kourtney didn't.

KHLOÉ: And you just popped him out!

KOURTNEY: I'm very mellow and my doctor was very mellow. He was the same one who delivered me and all of Mom's kids.

KHLOÉ: Kourtney is normally monotone. But when she was pregnant she became even more so. More chill.

KOURTNEY: Really? I feel like I got irritated a lot for some reason. I wasn't drinking, of course, and surprisingly, didn't miss it or feel left out at all. But being around drunk people really annoyed me.

KIM: It was so cool to see Kourtney warm up after she had Mason. She changed into a completely different person.

KOURTNEY: My friends who've had babies told me this, and it's true: You just become a different woman when you have a child. Your priorities are different. And when they're first born you are totally obsessed with them. You love staring at their little hands and feet. You think everything they do is cute. I remember one day I was kissing Mason and he spit up in my mouth and I loved it.

KHLOÉ: Kourtney, gross!

MASON'S FIRST CLOSE-UP

Kourtney: We weren't going to let Mason's birth be filmed. E! wanted cameras there. They must have asked about a hundred times and I kept saying, "Absolutely not!" I wanted it to be private.

So Scott home-videoed it. With Scott filming it wasn't invasive. It's not like I had a mic on or a lighting guy standing there. That would have been too weird. Then when we watched it, it was just amazing. But I was still nervous about giving it to E! because it was our footage, you know? It was such a personal moment, especially pulling Mason out.

In the end we decided to go ahead and let them air it. There were parts where I looked terrible, and I said, "Please, can you not show my face right there?" But then I said, "What do I care? I'm having a baby." I'm glad that we did share it. It was such a nice moment. We got all these responses that were so great. People were writing things like, "I didn't even cry when my niece was born, but I cried when Mason was born!"

But remember, E! did add music and all that.

ADDICTED TO LOVE

by Kim

My brother Rob and I are identical. We're the biggest hopeless romantics. It feels like we fall in love with everyone we meet. We think for sure they're the one and we're going to marry them. Of course, it doesn't always turn out that way. Obviously.

Kourtney is the opposite of a hopeless romantic. Whatever happens is fine. She doesn't have to be married. She just doesn't care.

Whereas I always think that I'll know the one I'm going to marry because he'll ride up to me on a white horse, with a princess crown and hand it to me! I'm literally like that, it's so crazy! I'm a relationship person, as opposed to a dater. I'm a long-term relationship girl.

I guess part of the reason I cry so much is that I'm such an incurable romantic. I love crying. When you're upset it's such a release. And the best thing in the world is to watch a really sad love movie and cry.

As I've gotten older, it's become more important for me to seek out the kind of man who would make a really good partner. So I'm getting to be a more sensible romantic.

I love a guy with a great smile. He has to make me laugh. And I like him to have a good sense of style, too, though if he doesn't, I know I can teach him. I also like guys who are motivated and driven. I don't care what he does but I want him to be passionate about it.

I want a guy who's fit, because it's important to me that I work out and be fit. That's my lifestyle. And I like a man who has a routine, and some structure in his life. I crave routine and I love to plan. I like to know the night

> I GUESS PART OF THE REASON I CRY SO MUCH IS THAT I'M SUCH AN INCURABLE ROMANTIC. I LOVE CRYING. WHEN YOU'RE UPSET IT'S SUCH A RELEASE.

before exactly what I'm doing the next day. Even on vacation I like to plan: Okay, we're gonna get up, we're going to get a massage, then we'll go here, and there . . .

I look for someone who's a good person: considerate, thoughtful, and with a big heart. For me, the guy who has everything is the one who just gives you a feeling of calmness. You have to always trust your gut.

But the most important thing to remember is that everyone comes into your life for a reason, a season, or a lifetime. Whether you just want to have fun with someone, or he's helping you get through a difficult time, or he's the one who'll be by your side forever, he's there for a reason. I'd like to believe that everyone has a soulmate, but maybe everyone has many. And along the way your soul connects to people who will be in your life to help you grow and teach you lessons.

Dashing to the Chapel

By Khloé

Lamar and I knew we wanted to marry each other within three or four days after we met. He actually asked my mom for my hand in marriage. It meant a lot to him to do that.

A few days before my wedding, I called up people and said, "Are you busy on Saturday? Save the date! Because I'm getting married that day." They'd say, "No you're not!" They had already heard on the news that I was getting married but they didn't know if it was real. I'd say, "Yes, I am!" I kept it playful because I wanted people to come. I didn't want to make it all serious, like, "I need your blessing," because already some people were wary about me getting married thirty days after I met the guy. What they probably don't realize is that I've been through a lot and even my family thinks of me as older than my years. My dad always said, "Out of all the kids, you I don't worry about. If I leave you on a street corner, you'll find your way."

I love any and every single wedding photo I have, but we had no idea that my mom had decided to send this out as our Christmas card. We were all saying, "Why the hell is Ryan Seacrest in our Christmas card?" — *Khloé*

I feel like Lamar was a gift from my dad. My defenses were up too high for me to be open to him on my own, and it's like someone else was forcing me to see. And there were so many weird coincidences that made me feel like Lamar and I were meant to be. We met on August 27 and we got married on September 27, which, okay, was on purpose. But then I had to send our marriage license in the mail to Social Security, to change my name

(I dropped my middle name and became Khloé Kardashian Odom). When they sent back my Social Security card, the date on it was January 27. And my favorite number has always been 7, and that's Lamar's jersey number.

The coolest thing was when we were flying to New York to go get my wedding dress and see Lamar's kids. My mother had asked us before, "If you could have anyone in the world sing at your wedding, who would it be?" And we said Stevie Wonder. So guess who happens to sit next to us on the flight to New York? Stevie Wonder. I was like, "Oh my God! This is another sign!" And also his assistant's name was Lamar.

We'd never seen Stevie Wonder before and we were so nervous. But we got to talking and he said he was a big Lakers guy and a huge fan of Lamar's. Blind people have extra senses, you know, and he said he could feel this aura of love and happiness around us. He couldn't perform at our wedding because of commitments with his kids, but he said, "Bless this marriage." Meeting him like that was even better than having him sing at the wedding.

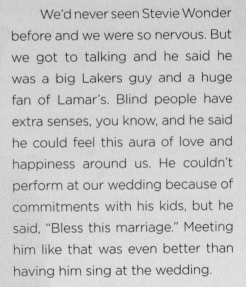

A few months after we got married, Lamar and I decided on the spur of the moment to get matching initial tattoos. Mine says LO (for Lamar Odom) on my right hand and his has KO (for Khloé Odom) on both hands—he says a man should always do more for a woman! — Khloé

The day of the wedding was incredible. There were so many hair and makeup people there we didn't know what was happening. It had all come together really fast, and there was only time to do one fitting for Kim's and Kourtney's bridesmaid dresses. Kim had wanted her dress to be really tight, and when she put it on, she could barely squeeze into it. She was freaked. She said, "I won't be able to sit down!" We're like, "Well, you look good, so just stand."

We didn't have time for a honeymoon right away so we planned it for later. Kim asked if she could come with us and I said of course. I knew it wouldn't mean she'd be with us every minute. Say we went to Fiji. Why would I care if Kim came along? What the hell are Lamar and I going to do in Fiji by ourselves anyway?

I don't go to church a lot, but I'm very spiritual and do read the Bible. Lamar and I pray together every night. If we're away from each other and on the phone, he says a prayer for both of us. Praying is our thing.

CALL ME KK

Khloé: When I got married, I became a stepmom to an adorable girl and boy. But I hate that word *stepmom*. It sounds mean and evil. I told them to call me "KK" instead. So now I'm a KK so I can be cool!

17

WE
MEAN
BUSINESS

Being a celebrity is fun, but it doesn't pay the bills.

Well, it does, in a way. It *can*. But only if you make good use of the opportunities it gives you. We're celebrities on the outside, but businesswomen to the core.

As you know by now, our parents practically tattooed "Work Ethic" on our foreheads when we were young. It's in our blood: We're absolutely committed to achieving success and financial security. While it's great to be photographed and fussed over, it's only so much fluff unless it's serving our greater goals. We take the business end of our business very seriously.

Or our businesses, we should say, because we've got a lot of them. The popularity of our shows on E! has led to all sorts of ventures—our own clothing line, jewelry, fragrance, diet supplements, skin care, just to name a few. We certainly don't jump at everything we're offered. No way. If we're going to be involved in something, we have to make sure it reflects our lifestyle and values. We have to truly believe in it.

And we don't participate in any enterprise unless we can be fully involved and ensure it meets our standards. We won't just sign our name to a product without knowing everything about it and providing our input.

Taking advantage of people is a bad thing; taking full advantage of opportunities is a good thing. We have a lot of fun doing *Keeping Up with the Kardashians* and it's also a perfect commercial for our products. We're trying to make the most of our current success and we don't apologize for it. We're paving our way to a future of continued and lasting success. That's what smart businesswomen do. Even if they're just in the business of pursuing their dreams.

Really, no matter whether you're on TV or working nine to five or studying in school, that's the business we're all in, right? Pursuing our dreams!

We've come up with some simple business guidelines that will help your dream ventures rock!

1. Capitalize on your opportunities.

That just means be alert to ways you can make the most of what you have or situations you're in. And then get to it! It's like when Kim's friends all wanted her to clean out their closets and then wondered what to do with the stuff they were getting rid of. Hello! She started a closet-organizing business. And since she was already putting up her own stuff on eBay, she realized she could make money doing that for other people, too.

But it doesn't have to be about money. Let's say you have musical talent. If you practice really hard and get accepted into a group that gets to travel to other cities to perform, that's maximizing your opportunities!

2. Get involved, and give it your all.

Don't just look for a quick money-making scheme that you think will run itself. Because it doesn't exist. And if it does, it's probably because it's a swindle, which is totally uncool and will ruin your reputation. (Remember, your reputation is the most valuable asset you have!)

Same thing if you're running a charity drive. How can you expect other people to put out the effort and convince people to give if you're not doing the same? The best ventures, business and otherwise, are the ones you are passionate about and work hard at. Those are the ones that will lead to success.

And btw, don't do anything halfway. Seriously, if you're going to do something, why wouldn't you do it all the way? Giving less than 100 percent is just a waste of your time and everyone else's.

3. ## Consider your options and take your time.

If you've got an important decision to make, don't rush it. It's fun to be spontaneous and all that, but with choices that have real consequences, allow yourself enough time to really think things through. Khloé doesn't always go along with this. Kim's pretty good at it. But Kourtney's really good at it. Sometimes to the point where you literally want to shake her until an answer falls out!

Kourtney: If you need a decision really quick, don't ask me. Ask the other two. Especially with really important decisions. I like to know all my options. That's just how I am. Even if I'm just going to make a purchase or something, I research it to death. I had to buy a new refrigerator and I looked at all of them, and analyzed everything. I wanted to buy the best one, you know? I remember it took so long for me to buy a chandelier for my dining room. Finally after a year with no chandelier my mom took me to a lighting fixture store. And right away I said, "This is the one." You just know when you know.

Part of it is that I'm just very laid-back, and I think things happen the way they're supposed to. For example, if I see a house I want to buy, my mom is like, "You better put in an offer right away!" No, if the house sells to someone else, then it's just meant to be. I take my time with things and they kind of fall into place.

Way before I had Mason my mom was pushing me and pushing me, telling me, "You've got to get a baby nurse right now!" I didn't even want a baby nurse. "But you have to have one!" I'm like, "I'm fine, I can do it myself. People used to live in caves and they managed on their own." Then about a month before Mason was born I met with this woman and I instantly liked her. It worked out perfectly. There's no point in stressing. It will all work out.

> PART OF IT IS THAT I'M JUST VERY LAID-BACK, AND I THINK THINGS HAPPEN THE *WAY* THEY'RE SUPPOSED TO.

4. Have an agenda.

That's kind of a play on words. In business, "having an agenda" can mean you've got something up your sleeve and you're trying to put one over on someone. But having an agenda can also mean that you have it clear in your mind what you want to accomplish and the steps you're going to take to make it happen. That we highly recommend.

An agenda can also mean an outline for a meeting with all the things you want to cover and agree on. Believe us, we come across that kind of agenda constantly because we have gazillions of meetings all the time. Meetings can be somewhat tiresome, but they're a fact of life in business. Agendas actually help you focus and get right to the important stuff.

And then an agenda is kind of an old-fashioned word for like, a day planner, which is actually another old-fashioned word for where you keep your schedule, whether it's on your BlackBerry or a little notebook in your purse or in your head or you've got it on PowerPoint. (If you've got it on PowerPoint, more power to you—you're obviously on the fast track, babe!)

What we're trying to say is that it's just really helpful to have a system that works for you in terms of scheduling. We could not get through one single day if we didn't manage to make order out of the chaos of our commitments and appointments and responsibilities. You may think that's why God made assistants, but get this: Kim, who is the most running-around, ridiculously efficient workaholic of any of us, doesn't even have an assistant! She's so good at scheduling she even schedules in time with friends.

5. Never flake out. And don't be late!

You simply cannot be taken seriously if you make a commitment and don't follow through. It's like the number-one rule of business. Listen, it happens to us all the time: We've promised to make a meeting or be at an event or whatever, and something else comes up that we'd much rather do. Whether it's a fun thing or something we really feel we should do, it doesn't matter. You can't ditch what you originally committed to.

Now, we admit that we don't always follow that rule in our personal lives, even though of course that would be ideal. But if it's business, you better make sure you're there, and on time. We hate, hate, hate being late. And we hate it when other people are, too. Honestly, if you don't want to totally get on our bad side, don't show up half an hour after you're supposed to!

Kim: I just feel like I can do my own scheduling better than anyone else. I mean, I know best where I need to be and how long it will take me to get there and everything I want to fit in. I'm good at wedging things into my day. For example, say I need to get my nails done for an event. If I've got an hour window between appointments, maybe I can have a house-call mani-pedi. I always try to think of how I can accomplish two things at once, as long as neither one of them requires my full concentration.

Sometimes I have to get creative to make sure I take care of not just my professional life but my personal life, too. I don't get to spend as much time with my friends as I'd like, so on my days off, I'll often have lunch twice. I meet one friend and have a little snack and then afterwards meet another friend and eat a little something else.

> I got invited to the 2010 White House Correspondent's Association dinner at the last minute and was freaking out because I had nothing to wear. My mom said she had a Valentino dress she bought in Paris in 1984 and I never thought it would fit me. But it was a perfect fit! She cried when she saw it on me. — *Kim*

Khloé: I have to make a confession. I didn't really want to do the second season of *Kourtney and Khloé Take Miami*. What can I say? I was a newlywed and I wanted to stay in L.A. and be with my husband. Kourtney really wanted to do it. Well, yeah, I thought, but she can take her family with her. In the end, though, I did it, because it was the right thing to do for many reasons. And in spite of my initial reluctance, I threw myself into it totally. I didn't hold back and you know what? We got a great season out of it!

217

6. Money matters—so pay attention.

Our parents tried to teach us responsibility when we were growing up. That included being smart about the way we handled money. It's so necessary to have a basic understanding of finance and especially credit. You can't really manage your own career or a household budget or your own spending money, for that matter, unless you're totally clued in to all that stuff. Of the three of us, Kourtney is the most frugal and responsible with her money. Khloé had to learn it the hard way.

See? Simple. Okay, girls. Now that you've learned Business 101, go get what you want!

Khloé: I really wish they would teach you about credit and other money-related stuff in school, because it's so important in life! It took me years to learn how to manage my finances. My dad was around to teach my sisters, but then he was gone and that kind of thing isn't really my mom's forte. I used to get credit card applications in the mail so I'd get all these cards and use them all over the place. But then I would forget about paying the bill. I would always be late, which costs you extra. I got myself into a bad situation.

It's hard to understand when you're young, but credit is actually worth more than money, and if you're not responsible with credit it can totally screw you up for the rest of your life. In the last couple of years I've cleaned my credit up and learned a lot. Now I'm totally on top of my finances. In fact, at home and for sure in my business, I make sure every bill comes through me.

K-TIP FROM KIM

HOW TO MASTER A KILLER SCHEDULE

◀ Write everything down. I'm very big on lists.

◀ Set alarms on your phone to remind you when you have to make a call or do something.

◀ When you have to be somewhere, allow extra time for traffic. Especially in L.A.

◀ If you feel yourself coming down with a cold and just can't afford to be sick, start downing Emergen-C right away and keep doing it. Also do this if someone around you is getting sick, so you won't catch it.

ON KARDASHIAN TIME

CHILL

To totally relax and pamper ourselves, we like to . . .

◄◄ KOURTNEY ►►

sleep without setting
an alarm clock

get a massage

take Mason on an adventure

◄◄ KIM ►►

get a massage

get a manicure and pedicure

work out

◄◄ KHLOÉ ►►

sleep in with my husband
and wake up whenever
we want

get a massage

get a manicure and pedicure

cook and eat dinner at home

have a hot bubble bath with
my husband and a side of
champagne and fruit

KHLOÉ: Kourtney is a little bad with timing.

KOURTNEY: What?

KHLOÉ: You're normally always late.

KOURTNEY: Well, I'm late sometimes now after I had a baby.

KHLOÉ: Oh come on, you were always late before that, too. Remember that one meeting when I started Twittering that my biggest pet peeve is when people are late, they do not respect my time?

KOURTNEY: I had a baby at the time.

KHLOÉ: No you didn't, you were pregnant!

KOURTNEY: I feel like in Miami people are always late for some reason, like they're never on a schedule. I'm just usually very much on a schedule.

KHLOÉ: Kourtney's always late. The rest of us aren't. We get it from our mom. Normally I'm never, ever late, and if I am, it's out of my control and I'm incredibly apologetic about it. It kills me when people are late and they don't even say a word about it. Like, you want to say you're sorry or something? Really, it kind of messes up the whole day.

REGIS AND KELLY AND KIM

Kim: I have never missed a flight. Never. Until . . . The very first flight that I missed was due to weather. I was in Los Angeles and had my fragrance launch at night and my flight was at seven the next morning. But there was a blizzard in New York City and the planes weren't taking off. I was like, "Well, I've gotta get there. I have *Regis and Kelly* in the morning." And after that I was co-hosting the *Today* show. I had all these things to do.

So I go, "Okay, where's the closest airport I can get to?" So I flew to Atlanta and then I flew to Boston—it took three stops. I asked to have a car waiting in Boston so I could drive down to New York. It was snowing all the way but I got there. Regis and Kelly couldn't believe I made it. They said, "We've had such a hard time booking anyone. Everyone else canceled—but you're here!"

Of course!

Kimberly

guacamole:
8 avacados (ripe)
1 jar of salsa (La Victoria/no chunky)
1 can sliced olives
green onions
tomatoes
sour cream
shredded cheddar cheese
lawyers season salt
lemon

mix avacado
salsa
seasonings
sprinkle lemon on top

Spinach Dip
frozen chopped spinach
shredded mozzerella
mayo
parmason cheese

KHLOÉ'S HONEY-GLAZED SALMON

I like to put honey on the salmon before it goes into the oven, then add more honey after it's cooked for extra flavor. The lemon adds a bit of tang.

◖ INGREDIENTS

4 Tbsp. light olive oil

4 Tbsp. softened butter

2 Tbsp. lemon juice

1 Tbsp. Lawry's seasoning salt

1 Tbsp. black pepper

2 Tbsp. honey

2 6-oz. salmon fillets

◖ DIRECTIONS

Preheat oven to 375 degrees. Skin and clean fillets. Pour half the light olive oil in a dish and spread evenly to keep the salmon from sticking. Place fillets in dish, drizzle remaining olive oil over them, then spread butter on top. Season with salt and black pepper. Drizzle with half the honey and bake for 35 to 45 minutes, until salmon is easily punctured with a fork. Remove from oven and drizzle remaining honey over salmon. Sprinkle with lemon juice. Enjoy!

TIME OUT

Kim: On mornings when I don't have to go to work I still get up no later than 9:00, even if I went to bed late. On my days off I like to work out. Shockingly, it really does make me feel better about myself. I also like to be lazy, and clean and organized. Sometimes I go shopping.

If I'm in a relationship, we might go out to dinner or the movies, or just hang out and play games. Or go bowling! One Christmas my boyfriend and I got custom bowling balls for everyone in the family. No matter what, I always spend time with my family when I have downtime.

And I cook, too. I make this amazing sweet potato puree!

Khloé: E! has us filming as much as possible. So some days I'm up at 3 A.M. and don't get home till 6 P.M. At night I don't want to miss anything so I fight to stay awake. I really try, but I usually fall asleep before I want to.

I love entertaining and having friends over. Every night I'm in town I try to cook dinner at home at least for Lamar and me and any family that's around. I can cook anything and I like to try different things. I make a lot of Italian, like Italian baked chicken, Italian sausage that I make with four colors of bell peppers, or pasta primavera. And I do a yummy honey-glazed salmon.

Kourtney: Before Mason, dinner out was the usual routine. Now we stay home a lot more and watch movies. We usually get take-out, or Scott and I will take Mason out to dinner. I actually can cook. I pretend that I can't so that I don't have to cook. But I do make all of Mason's food fresh in a baby food cooker.

THE PEAKS AND THE PITS . . . OF OUR LIVES

◄◄ KHLOÉ ►►

MY PEAKS are getting married, seeing the births of my little sisters, and seeing the birth of Mason.

THE PITS are my dad's death, and all the deaths I've experienced. Papa, my grandfather on my mom's side, passed before my dad, and then my dad's mom died just a few years after he did, because of her broken heart.

◄◄ KIM ►►

THE BIGGEST PEAK was a great childhood. It was just the best. And the greatest friends, ones I've known forever since even preschool and elementary school.

THE PITS have been annoying relationship stuff. I feel a hundred years old already, like I've been doing this dating stuff for so long!

◄◄ KOURTNEY ►►

MASON IS THE BIGGEST PEAK—the whole experience, the pregnancy, delivery, having a child now. Everything is totally positive.

THE BIGGEST PIT is Dad's death for sure. The divorce was a pit and the OJ trial was a pit.

◄◄ ►►

A BIG PEAK is right now, this period of our lives when we have a lot of great opportunities and blessings, and we get to spend a lot of time together. We're very lucky that our jobs are all intertwined so we're working together every day. And we own businesses together, travel together, and do very cool stuff.

We showed our first fashion line for Bebe at Fashion Week in New York. This dress is from our collection. — *Kim*

A KARDASHIAN CHRISTMAS

You may be wondering why we all of a sudden want to talk about Christmas, now, just as we get close to the end of the book. It's because Christmas is *huge* in the Kardashian family, and we wanted to save one of the best things for last.

Christmas is one of those times that we feel super, super close, and thankful to have each other. It's been so incredibly special to us for our whole lives that our story just wouldn't be complete if we didn't tell you about it. So just get in a sleigh bells and Santa Claus state of mind and indulge us for a minute, okay?

Kourtney: Christmas was definitely my favorite holiday. Mason's first Christmas was really great. Every year we have matching pajamas, and for that one it was Ralph Lauren plaids. Mom invited Scott's parents over and everyone got along and had a nice time. She gave Mason a kiddie-size electric Lamborghini. He could have cared less at the time because he was only eleven days old. But Scott was into it.

Ever since we were born, Mom had a party every year on Christmas Eve—and still does—and we have elves and Christmas carolers and the decorations are so over the top. After my parents went to bed, Kim and I would always get flashlights and try to peek over the banister, to see if we could see anything happening downstairs by the tree. Like Santa stopping by with our presents. In the morning, he'd always taken a bite of the cookies we left him, and a drink of milk.

Christmas is an incredibly huge deal at our house. By looking at our Christmas cards you can see how everyone in the family—and the clothes we wear!—have changed through the years.
— *Kourtney, Kim, and Khloé*

225

On Christmas morning we'd open presents with Mom and Bruce. Then we'd go to my dad's house for more presents, but he'd always read us the story of Christmas from the Bible before we could open presents.

I also love that Mason's birthday is right before Christmas because the energy and feeling I get at that time of year is so amazing. The Christmas music playing in stores and on the radio, the smell of Christmas everywhere, I just love it! When he was born my mom bought me a bunch of Christmas books for him and I read to him every night.

Kim: Christmas has definitely always been my favorite holiday. We each have our own stocking. My mom decorates the entire house starting after Thanksgiving, and every year our tree has a theme, and there are so many presents! She always has a big Christmas Eve party. Santa would come—sometimes my dad dressed up as Santa—and we were always begging to go see the reindeer. We believed in Santa for a really long time.

We always woke up at five or six on Christmas morning and got our parents up. My mom says her first memory of me and Kourtney waking them up on Christmas morning was me so excited and full of energy. I was

Peace, Love and Joy....
Merry Christmas from The Jenners !!!
Bruce, Kris, Kourtney, Kimberly, Khloe
Robert, Kendall and Kylie

like, "Hurry! Get up! I can't wait!" But Kourtney was so blasé about the whole thing. She didn't even really care about the presents. "Can I have my breakfast now?" she asked.

One Christmas I cried because Kourtney got something I wanted. I can't remember what I asked for, but I got a fish tank instead. It was so unfair. That used to happen to me a lot. I wanted a particular watch when I graduated from high school and I kept

Someone took a picture of me and Nicole Richie at one of my mom's Christmas parties. I remember it was an extremely fun Christmas! — *Kim*

asking for it the whole year. And then Kourtney, who was a year ahead of me in school, graduated and got my watch! The very same one. She didn't even know about the watch until then. I think my parents were just lazy, and I kept giving them good ideas.

So back to Christmas. After my parents were divorced, we'd usually go to our dad's house in the afternoon. And then we'd eat dinner Christmas night with Khloé's godparent, the boxer Sugar Ray Leonard, and his wife at their house.

My most memorable Christmas was probably one year when we were older. It was in the morning and we were doing the tree and suddenly my dad walks in. We were like, "What are you doing here?" So he throws a set of keys to Khloé and says, "Go look outside." He was giving her a brand-new Mercedes! She was so surprised and excited. We all were!

2005

Khloé:
Christmas is my favorite holiday. For my mom's party every Christmas Eve we'd each have to dress according to a theme. One year we had to wear something with a Burberry pattern. One year ball gowns were popular so we had to wear ball gowns. I don't know who came up with those rules but I'm so glad we don't have to do that anymore.

All our Christmases were amazing but one of the most memorable was when, let's see, I must have been seventeen. For my sixteenth birthday my parents had given me my dad's old black Tahoe and I was really pissed, because Kim and Kourtney had both gotten new cars when they turned sixteen. I thought, is this a joke? Being an ungrateful teenager, I thought they were mistreating me or maybe punishing me for being a bad girl, which I was in those days. Later I realized my parents had just learned their lesson after my sisters crashed their cars two months after they got 'em: Don't give a sixteen-year-old a brand-new car.

We always spent Christmas morning with my mom and Bruce at their house. On this one Christmas morning, all of sudden we see Dad walking up to the house. We were so surprised.

It's a Christmas tradition at our house to wear matching pajamas when we open our presents. — *Kourtney*

So he gives me a little heart-shaped box with a single key inside it. Everyone started screaming. We went outside and there was a silver Mercedes C-class. Dad explained he'd ordered a black one, but it was late and still on the truck, so the silver one was just sitting in for the real one. I said, "No! I want this one!" This time, I was totally appreciative.

It was so funny, though, how excited everyone got. It was like everyone was getting a car!

That's kind of amazing—we all wrote about our Christmas memories separately. And yet we all picked the same Christmas as our most memorable! It was definitely a great surprise to see our dad on Christmas morning, but we were all so seriously excited about Khloé getting a new car. The thing is, when one of us is happy, we all feel happy. It's like "all for one and one for all!"

If you want to know our biggest secret, the true secret of our success, that's it. We're all in this together.

We feel very protective of our little sisters Kylie (she's the little one with the bow in her hair) and Kendall. And we're protective of Rob, too! — Kourtney, Kim, and Khloé

18

HAPPILY EVER AFTER

We've talked about boys, babies, business, growing up, school, clothes and makeup and hair, our mom, our dad, Bruce, and even Christmas.

So what are we missing? Actually we're missing a "who," not a "what." Three "whos," to be exact. (Enough, we're starting to sound like Dr. Seuss.)

We've been so focused on ourselves, we three sisters, that we haven't spent much time yet talking about our other siblings, our fabulous baby brother and our beautiful little sisters. Rob first.

No matter how old Rob gets, he'll always be our baby brother. Ever since he was born, all of us girls wanted to baby him. We're all so maternal. It was only natural—he was the only boy in the family and he was the youngest, three years younger than the youngest of us. He really was the baby! Our dad's name was Robert so people called Rob "Baby Robert." In fact, they called him that until he was fifteen. Poor guy. Finally people started saying, "You know, we can't call him Baby Robert forever." So he became Rob, much to his relief.

Rob will always be younger than we are, and as you know, boys are "younger" than girls in general, as in less mature. And since he's been around all these girls who pamper him his whole life, he's used to being our baby. Let's face it, he loves it.

KIM: Although he didn't like it at all when we were kids, we used to dress him up like a girl. We tortured him and teased him so much.

KHLOÉ: I remember the two of us used to play Barbie together, until Dad found out and he told Rob, "You cannot play with Barbies! You have to play with G.I. Joe!"

All the siblings in the family, except for Kendall and Kylie, have switched around and lived with different siblings at various times. So Rob has lived with all three of us.

KIM: It was easy having Rob at my house because he's just as obsessed with being neat and organized as I am.

KOURTNEY: Rob was living at my house after our dad died, when he was in high school. I had to make his bag lunches, but there was never any food in the house. So his lunches would be something like peanut butter and jelly with a stale English muffin or whatever I could find. A blueberry muffin from the week before.

KHLOÉ: Ooh, she is so gross.

KOURTNEY: All he ever did back then was play video games with my boyfriend, who was obsessed with them. Rob would stand outside Best Buy all night long and wait for the new video game to come out.

KHLOÉ: Oh, he's totally into video games now, too! He's living with me now. So I cook dinner every night, and every night he asks, "Can I bring my friends J.J. and Jesse over for dinner?" So I say okay and then my place turns into a frat house—I'm feeding his friends and he plays video games until 4 A.M. That's when I wake up and go in and say, "Honestly, you have to go to work in the morning. Go to sleep!" Rob needs a reminder to go to work every day. I need to literally tell Rob when I get up, "Okay, you're going to work, right? Go to the gym and then go to work!"

KOURTNEY: He's so lazy. Remember when he used to call us and ask us to make his dentist appointments?

KHLOÉ: And he was already over the age of eighteen. He'd start with Kim and go down the line. We'd be like, "No way!"

KIM: He's very needy.

KHLOÉ: But I do love having him around. Sometimes it's fun to hear all this noise in the house. And it's so sweet, we do The Peak and the Pit at dinner a lot, because he likes that kind of stuff.

As you can tell, we adore Rob. He's a really good guy. We grew up being around a lot of people and it's nice that we can experience that now with our baby brother.

Even though we'll never stop babying Rob—he'll never escape our clutches!—Kendall and Kylie are a different matter. Of course, we mother them, too. It's like instead of one mother they've had four.

Kendall 3&

Sister Khloé

There are many people that I like to spend time with, but the one how I mostly like to spend time with is my older sister Khloé. She loves to biy stoff and mostly she likes to biy puppies real puppies. Khloé loves to sope, and she is good at it too. When she went shoping one day she saw a little puppy and she bote it, she named it Booda. When me and my little sister Kylie saw Booda we thoght Booda was so cute. Khloé is so loving whenever I'm sick she calls the house and assks "are you ok? I would sometimes say yes but sometins I would say no. When Khloé got a dog named Harly for christmas a cople years later we had to give her away, because we were movind to a house with a small backyard. When Khloé is babysiting and me or kylie get hert she runs over to were we are and fixs wats rong. I think Khloé is so helpful.

She always helps me with my homework if she is there. When I am walking with Khloé and there is an elderly person she helps them acros the street. Somctims I cant reach something and then Khloé comes and get it down for me. When I cannt find something Khloé helps me.

Khloé is so silly. She maks me laphe so hard because she is so silly. I think she is the sillyist pedon ever. Khloé even makes my mom laphe because of her joks. Khloé is normily really funny but somctimes she is not funny.

Thats wiy I like Khloé.

> I never knew at the time that Kendall wrote this about me, for a third grade homework assignment. My mom got it back after she turned it in. I'm in love with it and I've saved it forever. Kendall and Kylie are like my babies. I would die for them! — *Khloé*

233

I was at my mom's house helping Kendall and Kylie with their home-work and I just decided to snap some pictures. I maybe have ten different silly faces from this night. They're from a vintage camera that Kourtney bought me that I keep with me all the time. — *Khloé*

But they're growing up so fast! Kendall already has a huge modeling career, which is so exciting. We thought about it for a year before she started, and right away she was doing modeling jobs almost every day. They asked her to do Fashion Week in New York and we said no, because we didn't want her traveling that far. But she's really enjoying it.

Kylie is anxious to do something of her own like Kendall, and she will soon enough. Kylie's two years younger, but she's a little bit faster than Kendall. She's very comfortable with her body and she's more into boys. We try to talk to both our little sisters about growing-up things, like their bodies and boys and sex and what you have to watch out for, but we're a little more vocal with Kylie because we don't want her going too fast. We really are like mothers, or even like Bruce: We kinda wish Kendall and Kylie wouldn't date at all!

No, seriously, we want them to have fun and enjoy their youth and eventually meet wonderful guys. There's so much to learn and go through. We would really love to spare them from making their own mistakes along the way, since we've already made them and they could learn from our example. Actually, it would be great if we could do that for everyone like Kendall and Kylie.

We guess that will never happen, because as we know from our own experiences, girls will be girls. We each have to find our own way.

Still, we can't resist trying. We had such a fantastic upbringing, and so many great things happened to us—and we learned so much the hard way. We care and we want to share. So we've written a letter to Kendall and Kylie and it's for all of you to read, too.

Dear Kendall and Kylie,

As you get older, you'll be more and more involved in all the drama that's just a natural part of our family. In fact, we're pretty sure it won't be long until you're the ones instigating most of the drama! We want you to have amazing lives and be at least as happy as we've been. So listen up.

Number one, you're beautiful, even without makeup. But don't base your whole self-image on the way you look. The way you feel is much more important. All the running around and sports that you do—keep it up.

Treat other people the way you want to be treated. Don't look down on someone for the way they dress or talk or how much money they have. And be compassionate and giving to people who aren't as fortunate as you.

Give Mom and Bruce a break. When you're young it's hard to see that your parents are looking out for your best interests. It may seem like they're being stubborn and unfair and old-fashioned, and maybe they are, but when you grow up you'll see how often they were right and you were wrong. And you'll be grateful for what they taught you, believe it or not.

When you're online, just try to be a little bit careful. Okay, we can't even imagine what it must be like to grow up with Twitter and Facebook and everything. We didn't even have cell phones when we were your age! But we know it's easy to get lulled into thinking you're safe when you're not. Don't trust just anybody out there. And remember that

This is Kylie with the love of her life, Dolce, a chihuahua. (We also have a black lab named Gabbana.) She is obsessed with this puppy! He only sleeps in her room. — *Khloé*

when you post something, everyone can see it and pass it around and it may be up there forever. So don't say things or show things you could be embarrassed about later.

Try to have confidence, and when you can't muster the real thing, fake it, baby! Guys can make it hard to feel confident. Not that they mean to, necessarily. But they're so different from girls, and they're generally not as evolved as we are. At the very least we can definitely say it takes longer for them to grow up. You may want to give yourself over emotionally to a guy, but he might not be ready to appreciate it. And no guy is worth changing yourself for. Be proud of who you are, and brave.

Don't let yourself be pressured by your friends, and especially your boyfriends. Everyone your age is in the process of finding out who they are, and what might be right for one person isn't right for everyone. If you're not comfortable doing something, don't do it. It doesn't matter who thinks you should or what they say about you. Be true to yourself. (And yes, we are talking about sex and fooling around!)

Speaking of sex, in fact, absolutely take Khloé's advice and don't have any until you're much older. Also take Kim's advice and don't get married when you're still a teenager.

We were doing a photo shoot at my mom's house and we got bored waiting for our turn so Kendall and I took some snapshots. I think Kendall looks gorgeous here. —*Khloé*

Never allow yourself to be mistreated. Especially by a boy, even if you really, really, *really* like him. As a bonus, in the long run it will make guys like you more.

After growing up in this family, surely you already know you're expected to work hard and be responsible. But just to remind you: We knew our fairy tale wouldn't last unless we got busy and made the effort to keep it going. Same goes for you, no matter how much you think you can twist Bruce around your little fingers.

When you make mistakes, try to learn from them. Yes, you will make mistakes. You'll date the wrong guy or do stupid, embarrassing things, or both. But remember that everything in life has something to teach us. The crisis will pass, and your family will help you get through it.

Random texts saying "I love you" to people you care about are always a good idea.

Kylie and I were having a blast dressing up together." — *Kim*

Almost last, but certainly not least, ALWAYS look up to your big sisters! Seriously, we do want you to adore us and admire us forever. But we don't want you to think you have to be us. Or be like us. We want you to be yourselves. Be comfortable in your own skin, which is a kind of weird way of saying be totally cool with who you are.

We hope you achieve fabulous, incredible things in your lives—but always remember what's truly important. We feel really blessed that so much amazing stuff is happening to us. And we're having a blast with it all. But if it ever stops being fun, or simply goes away, we'll just snap back to our normal lives, the lives we had before we became "The Kardashian Sisters." And we'll be completely, blissfully happy. Because the most important thing about being the Kardashian sisters . . . is being sisters.

Fame and fortune and even friends can all come and go. But family is forever.

Love,
Kourtney, Kim, Khloé

P.S.
OUR FAVES

FAVORITE COLORS

KOURTNEY:

Pink
Black
Red
"It changes all the time."

KIM:

White
Silver
Gold
"I don't like pink as much as
    everyone thinks."

KHLOÉ:

Purple
"I always loved purple, even
    before I knew it was a
    Lakers color."

FAVORITE TV SHOWS

KOURTNEY:

Lost

Oprah

Sex and the City

Snapped

Divine Design

American Idol

Beverly Hills 90210 (the original)

Punky Brewster

Saved by the Bell

KIM:

Sex and the City

Oprah

Forensic Files

KHLOÉ:

Hoarders

Crime 360

Snapped

Cheaters

Friends

Family Guy

*Seinfeld "My dad always
    watched and now I do, too."*

Sex and the City

Saved by the Bell

The Fresh Prince of Bel-Air

The Cosby Show

I Love Lucy

The Honeymooners

FAVORITE MAGAZINES

KOURTNEY:

Elle Decor

Elle

Harper's Bazaar

Architectural Digest

Italian Vogue

KIM:

Elle

Harper's Bazaar

Vogue

KHLOÉ:

Elle Decor

Architectural Digest

Vogue

Elle

FAVORITE WEB SITES

KOURTNEY:

habituallychic.com
babycenter.com
netaporter.com
google.com

KIM:

netaporter.com
perezhilton.com
shopbop.com

KHLOÉ:

netaporter.com
shopbop.com

FAVORITE BOOKS

KOURTNEY:

What to Expect the First Year
Domicilium Decoratus
The Prayer of Jabez
The Bible
The Catcher in the Rye

KIM:

Tuesdays with Morrie
The Purpose-Driven Life

KHLOÉ:

The Bible
The Coldest Winter Ever
The 48 Laws of Power

FAVORITE MOVIES

KOURTNEY:

Troop Beverly Hills
Breakfast at Tiffany's
My Fair Lady
Funny Face
Cary Grant movies
Bette Davis movies
Almost any old movie.
   "Old movies have such
   great stories!"

KIM:

The Notebook
Clueless

KHLOÉ:

Troop Beverly Hills
Welcome to the Doll House
Gentlemen Prefer Blondes
How to Marry a Millionaire
Some Like It Hot
Pillow Talk
Bye Bye Birdie
Moulin Rouge (the one
   by Baz Luhrman)
Love Story
Newsies

FAVORITE RECORDING ARTISTS

KOURTNEY:

Michael Jackson

"MJ will always be my fave."

Ne-Yo

Beyoncé

Black Eyed Peas

Michael Bublé

Lady Gaga

Stevie Wonder

DeBarge

Madonna

KIM:

J-Lo

Alicia Keys

Usher

Taylor Swift

Lady Gaga

Beyoncé

KHLOÉ:

Donny Hathaway

Anita Baker

Aretha Franklin

Lenny Kravitz

FAVORITE SONG

KOURTNEY:

"Pretty Young Thing"
Definitely something by
Michael Jackson.

KIM:

Anything by Beyoncé

KHLOÉ:

Donny Hathaway's version of
"For All We Know"